Whispers *of* *the* Lo Shu Grid

Lipiie Banerjjee

Dedicated to...

Each one of you reading this book and the cosmic relationships between each of us

Copyright © 2025 by Lipi Banerjjee

All rights reserved.

No portion of this book may be reproduced in any form without written permission from the publisher or author, except as permitted by Canadian copyright law.

Contents

1. VIBRATIONS & HISTORY OF EVOLUTION OF NUMEROLOGY — 1
2. BIRTHDATES & THEIR CHARACTERISTICS — 9
3. HISTORY OF LO SHU GRID — 19
4. MEANING OF NUMBERS AND THEIR ELEMENTARY RELATION — 25
5. HOW TO USE LO SHU GRID — 29
6. ARROWS — 35
7. REPETITIVE NUMBERS — 46
8. MISSING NUMBERS — 53
9. ANALYZING TWO LO SHU GRIDS FOR COMPATIBILITY — 58
10. PERSONAL YEARS — 63
11. SOME OTHER IMPORTANT NUMBERS HOUSE, VEHICLE, & MOBILE — 72
12. KUA NUMBER — 80

13.	MEANING OF KUA NUMBERS	84
14.	FENGSHUI BAGUA MAP & ITS EFFECTS	102
15.	PERSONAL YEAR GRID	106
16.	REMEDIES	109
17.	NUMBER COMBINATIONS	116
18.	About the Author	119

Chapter One

VIBRATIONS & HISTORY OF EVOLUTION OF NUMEROLOGY

"Everything in life is a vibration." - Albert Einstein

The Vibrations:

I would like to share my journey in "numerology," or the study of numbers, with you. I have been attracted to occult sciences for as long as I can remember. Those days I didn't know they were categorized as such. My primary interest then was Palmistry. On one of my summer vacations, I discovered a small book, Cheiro's Palmistry: the book of Fate and Fortune, in my Dad's small library. And I was hooked.

After grade 10, my hostel journey began. Along with that, my palmistry consultancy. Pro bono goes without saying. Though, I was quite sought after in those days. All the seniors started flocking around me. I say seniors as my fellow hostel mates were busy being ragged. One would think I was spared from ragging, isn't it? Alas, that was not the case. It was a time-out policy wherein I was consulted in between getting ragged. Can you imagine this?

As time passed, I got busy with my studies. One fateful night my father passed away, and life took a U-Turn. I shelved this passion of mine and tried to shoulder my newly imposed responsibilities. Many years went by, and I got married and had children. I still had that small book by Cheiro. One day, my husband got another book, Cheiro's Numerology & Astrology. Again, my old interest was piqued. I started reading the book. This was my first foray into Numerology and Astrology. Unfortunately, except for the number attributes, I couldn't understand much.

In 2003, I got my hands on another book, Instant Numerology, by Sandra Kovac Stein. It is a practical workbook. With the help of this book, I could interpret my chart very easily. Then I interpreted many more charts, and my confidence grew. Then came my first numerology mentor and everything changed for good. She dispelled whatever hesitation I had about deep diving into this subject. My enthusiasm grew with leaps and bounds, and I am very hopeful of infecting all the readers with my enthusiasm.

Now, you will also discover your numbers in the upcoming chapters, along with the numbers of your friends and family, and you will discover what each number symbolizes. You will learn how numbers (or vibrations) impact your job, sentiments, and personality. If you already have a relationship, you will be able to determine your compatible numbers, which will help you better understand them. If not, you will learn how to find a spouse who is compatible with you. You will discover each number's virtues and shortcomings. You will be astounded at how simple it is to effect the direction of your life since each of us has the capacity of free will to change the course of our destinies for better or worse. There are so many things that you can learn about each number. You'll discover the significance of colors and how they impact our lives. The following chapters will tell you which days of the week benefit your number and what jewels resonate with it.

You will learn how to choose the appropriate dwelling number and vehicle based on its number. "Remember, numbers reveal vibrations, and vibrations are the basis of all existence," This life of ours has a "pulse," and if we just stop for a second, we can feel it. You can grasp this numerology technique I'm writing about if you think in terms of vibrations. You will discover the importance of your name and what it symbolizes and learn to anticipate the outcome of specific events. You can plan your life more easily if you attentively follow each step.

Ever since the middle of the VIth Century, B.C., when Pythagoras gave the ancient Greeks his system of numbers, each succeeding age has been attracted, more or less, to his philosophy.

Each generation down the millennia has found the concept intriguing yet fantastical. Some people are aware of its accuracy. According to the old master's teaching, everything is in a state of vibration. The greater the rate of vibration, the more spirit force an object contains and the more positive its nature. The slower the rate of vibration, the less force it has and the more negatively it acts.

Before we continue, let me briefly explain why numbers are so important to us. The proverbs "his number was up" and "my days are numbered," among others, are ones we have all heard. Look around you at all the numbers; one is your house or apartment number. You will have a bank account number, a credit card number, a medical insurance number, and so on. There are numbers all around you that vibrate without your knowledge, but each has a function to play in life and pulses to its beat.

We rely on numbers today more than at any other moment in history. Computers are a reality, and they keep so much data in them that, at times, we are more of a number than a name. Whether we want it or not, we are constantly tracked by numbers "from the cradle to the cemetery." Have you ever needed to provide identification to someone? If so, what was the situation? Did you notice that the individual attempting to verify your identification was satisfied when he received something with a number on it, even though your name was sufficient? You are starting to understand what I mean when I say that since numbers play such a significant part in our lives, they shouldn't be taken for granted. In the following chapters, I'll offer you as much knowledge about numbers as possible so you can comprehend the vibrations in your life. Understanding how to balance your numbers will enable you to balance your life.

I wrote this book partly to dispel people's misconceptions about numbers. We may live more comfortably if we have a framework for understanding our life. The book shows the simplest of techniques; typically, the most fundamental concepts in life are the most difficult to understand. I do not doubt that anyone who puts the system to the test will be amazed by the outcomes in a very short amount of time. Our lives will be in harmony if our numbers are harmonious (remember, numbers are a clue to the vibrations around us). So come along on a journey with me into the realm of numbers.

History of Evolution of Numerology:

Numerology is as old as human civilization. Every human civilization has its numerology system, which was present with them and later either vanished or was rediscovered in a different form. The earliest traces of numerology evolution can be dated back to the late bronze age (Vedic Period (i.e., 4th – 6th Century BC)

The oldest direct reference to modern-day numerology can be found as old as the 1300s, and indirect references are even older.

There is no need to compare two systems of numerology or two branches of occult sciences, as each has its attributes, pros, and cons.

Some of the Numerology systems

• Chaldean Numerology: Attributed to Babylonians. They did not consider the number nine while assigning a number to the alphabet. Nine is considered a sacred number; its attribute is "giving" and "humanity". The ancients (including me and many others) believed that these attributes we learn as we grow and evolve.

• Pythagorean Numerology: Attributed to Pythagoras of Samos & Philolaus (Researcher from Pythagorean Community)

• Lo Shu Grid Numerology: Having inspiration from Yantras of Agam Granthas and attributed to South East Asian Countries of the modern day world.

Numerology has a long history that dates back thousands of years. Numerology was employed by the Chinese, Japanese, Greeks, Hebrews, Egyptians, Phoenicians, early Christians, Mayans, and Incas to understand various subjects, including the universe and themselves. Chaldean numerology differs significantly from one of the better-liked systems, Western Numerology, credited to Pythagoras (c. 500 BCE).

Instead of sound vibrations, the Pythagorean system is based on sequential patterns. The alphabet is listed in alphabetical order beneath a numbering system that ranges from 1 to 9.

One notable exception is the number 9. The ancient Chaldeans held this number in the highest regard; hence they did not include it in the number chart; however, they did include it as a name total. This number was revered by the ancients, probably in part because of its relationship to infinity (it is the only number that can be multiplied by any other number and always return to its original value), but Pythagoras paid it little attention, even giving its domain the letters I and R. Furthermore, Chaldean numerology only considers the name you are presently using, as opposed to the birth or given name because it is those energies that are affecting you right now rather than those you held in the past. Name changes are another factor to take into account here. Names may change, changing energy vibrations, whether by necessity or choice- adoption, marriage, divorce, or even the creation of nicknames.

The easiest occult art to comprehend and apply is numerology. To uncover all the mysteries the numbers contain, you only need the person's full name and birth date. (Most experts concur that all computations regarding names must be performed using your full birth name as it appears on your birth certificate). However, Chaldean experts believe in using the birth certificate and the more widely used or known name. Chaldean use sound vibration.

To create Numerology charts, eleven numbers are utilized. 1, 2, 3, 4, 5, 6, 7, 8, 9, 11, and 22 are the numbers in question. You keep reducing the numbers until you have a single digit or the "master" numbers 11 or 22. These numerical values each stand for various traits and expressions.

The lone exception to the general norm of reducing to a single digit are the master numbers. They are not reduced to single digits. The single- digit number that the master numbers 11 and 22 replace are intensified versions of that number (2 and 4). These figures point to the possibility of significant learning and/or achievement, frequently in a more demanding setting.

In a numerology chart, the results of multiple calculations are presented rather than only focusing on one specific number. The relationships between these statistics are then looked at and analyzed. Numerology is also quite easy to understand.

You can actually "do it yourself" because it is so easy.
LET'S GET GOING!

Primary Figures Extracted from the Birth Date:

The Life Path Number, Expression Number, Soul Desire/Urge Number, and Personality Number are among the fundamental numbers generated from the date of birth. The sum of the birth date is used to calculate the life path number. It depicts a person's life path or the challenges and possibilities put in front of them. This secondary number is thought to be very important in later life.

Birth date: 15 November 1980

15+11+1980 = 1+5+1+1+1+9+8+0 = 26/8

8 is the Life Path number.

The soul urge number reflects a person's inner motivations and desires. It is derived from the name's total vowel sound.

A person's personality number represents their external demeanor and the impression they give off to others. It is generated from the name's consonant count. This number represents a person's potential for success and accomplishment in life.

Birth Compound Number: This number applies to anyone born after the ninth day of any month.

The two-digit birth dates have their significance, influence, and meaning.

For instance:

Birth date: November 15, 1980

Birth Number: 1 + 5 = 6

15 is the birth compound no.

Chapter Two

BIRTHDATES & THEIR CHARACTERISTICS

"Number Rules the Universe." - *Pythagoras*

1st of the Month:
Individuals born on the 1st of the month benefit from pure one energy. They acquire reason, drive, excitement, independence, and analytical skills. They are likely to suppress their feelings out of concern that they will appear weak. They naturally take on leadership roles and relish chances to show off their abilities.

2nd of the Month:
Individuals born on the 2nd of the month are warm, loving, giving, romantic, sentimental, perceptive, and on occasion, moody. They frequently experience anxiety. They occasionally get depressed and require the ongoing support of others. They would rather collaborate with others than operate alone.

3rd of the Month:

Individuals born on the 3rd of the month are typically very well-liked and extroverted, imaginative, gregarious, communicative, and show all the delights of life. They frequently ideate better than they execute. They usually have multiple significant relationships throughout their lives and are restless. They have a gift for language and will probably do best in any occupation where they can use it: teaching, consulting, and sales.

4th of the Month:

Individuals born on the 4th of the month tend to be organized and appreciate a challenge. They also deeply lovetheir families, homes, and nations. They are diligent, willing to put in much effortand wait patiently for what they want.

5th of the Month:

Individuals born on the 5th of the month areadaptable and extroverted with a freelifestyle. They lack focus as they continuously learn new things.These folks frequently succeed in business. They are intelligent, gregarious, social, and well-adjustedindividuals.

6th of the Month:

Individuals born on the 6th of the month tend to be optimistic, kind, and humanitarian.

In general, they are happiest while assisting others. They relish the obligations of marriage and parenthood. They don't hesitate to express their emotions to others.

7th of the Month:

Individuals born on the 7th of the month are perceptive, sensitive, and like to solve problems on their own. They prefer working alone while conducting research and studying.

Though harboring deep emotions, tenderness is difficult to express and receive for them.

8th of the Month:

Individuals born on the 8th of the month make excellent business people. They love dealing with money and the financial world and have great ideas for money-making. They possess ambition, drive, and commonsense and are willing to put in a lot of effort to achieve their goals as long as they believe the goals are worthwhile.

9th of the Month:

Individuals born on the 9th of the month are naturally compassionate, yet they frequently suffer because other people don't appreciate what they do. They frequently find themselves in abusive marriages and relationships, giving much more than they receive. Number nine people are happiest working in creative fields and have vivid imaginations. They are optimistic, tolerant, and open-minded.

10th of the Month:

Individuals born on the 10th of the month tend to be highly motivated, imaginative, and skilled salespeople. They are adept at juggling multiple tasks at once and frequently need to be coerced into taking time off to unwind. Independent, aspirational, and self-assured, they are born to lead.

11th of the Month:

Individuals born on the 11th of the month are stubborn, authoritative, and rebellious. In many occult traditions, it is called a "mystic number". They are positive, quick to act, and can lead themselves and others with their inspirational ideas. They change their minds often, get separated from their partners, and have frequent ups and downs in their feelings. Those who were born on the 11th of any month often have brilliant ideas, but they are rarely able to see them through to completion. Although these individuals possess exceptional intuition and talent, their anxiety and tense personalities make it difficult to accomplish their objectives.

12th of the Month:

Individuals born on the 12th of the month benefit from both the energies of 1 (Sun) and 2 (Moon).Compared to persons born on the third of the month, they are more complex, swinging between extremes; cheerful, optimistic, understanding, and humane at onetime and exactly the opposite at other times. Careless about others' feelings, they often embellish reality and persuade others to agree with them and their thoughts. They make delightful, entertaining, and knowledgeable conversationalists.

13th of the Month:

Individuals born on the 13th of the month have the combination of 1 (Sun) and 3 (Jupiter), giving an irritable nature. This number indicates changes in one's plans and place but is not as unfortunate as it is made out to be. It is a number of alert, practical and dependable people. Those who were born on the thirteenth of the month are diligent, methodical, and have great potential for achievement. They use caution and are steadfast, disciplined, and tenacious. They can easily go to the depth of matters.

14th of the Month:

Individuals born on the 14th of the month are adventurous, bold, adaptive, and open-minded. It is a karmic compoundof 1

(Sun) and 4 (Rahu). Rahu partially eclipses the Sun and causes difficulties. Number14 people suffer from inner conflicts. Fourteen-borns should guard against natural calamities. They are intuitive by nature. Refraining from alcohol, drugs, and excessive sex will do them well. When necessary, they may work incredibly hard and enjoy working with others, but rarely put in lengthy hours.

15th of the Month:

Individuals born on the 15th of the month have intellect, ready wit, material success, literature, fine arts, and popularity. These people are also loyal and understanding. Having an innate sense that when someone needs a shoulder to lean on, they are the first ones to provide the same. They are affectionate, gregarious, and amiable, yet desire to maintain a certain level of independence.

16th of the Month:

Individuals born on the 16th of the month are idealists outwardly and lovers of enjoyment inwardly. They struggleto communicate their ideas and emotions, and instead of putting themselves in potentially uncomfortable circumstances, they frequently choose to withdrawinto themselves. Moreover, they struggle to show and receive love and affection. As they develop a solid faith andphilosophy of life, they graduallydevelop an interest in technical orscientific issues and enjoy researching and coming to their own conclusions.

17th of the Month:

Individuals born on the 17th of themonth have an aptitude for financial success and are steadfastly committed to achieving theirobjectives. Seventeen has an innerconflict, but this conflictgives rise to self-introspection and makespeople more aware, loving,and considerate towardsothers. Though encountering setbacks, they always succeed in getting what they desire. Self-assured, dependable, and practical, are adept at managing complicated projects.

18th of the Month:
Individuals born on the 18th of the month face intense inner conflict, opposition, obstacles, and strife in life. This number gives family feuds, enmities, betrayal from friends, and no peace and happiness. But they face challenges and adverse situations boldly.

19th of the Month:
Individuals born on the 19th of the month are associated with responsibility, ideals, and ambition. Because their emotions always triumph over logic, they occasionally let themselves down. It is a very lucky number showering happiness and success on the native. They are adaptable and prefer to operate independently with the least amount of outside disturbance, putting in a lot of effort and long hours.

20th of the Month:
Individuals born on the 20th of the month are impatient, nervous, shy, and dependent. They favour tranquil lifestyles and try to stay away from the bustle of modern life as much as possible. They frequently write effectively to convey their point of view. Married life may not be all that successful.

21st of the Month:
Individuals born on the 21st are associated with intelligence, humor, and creativity. Nonetheless, those born on this date are jittery, moody, and frequently worried over little things. They

may be in the best of spirits one moment and depressed the next. Possessor of strong linguistic abilities with a strong chance to succeed in any voice-related profession. They are generally kind, loving, generous, and diplomatic and destined to achieve name, fame, and popularity. In spite of being very suspicious and dominating their fantastic luck, fortune sees them through all walks of life happily and successfully.

22nd of the Month:

Individuals born on the 22nd are very capable but experience significant ups and downs in their life. They must suffer separation from family and loved ones, and many remarry. They can typically do considerably more in later life than most individuals will. They are extremely intuitive but prone to anxiety. This number is considered mystical by many. They are very obstinate people and are considered very difficult by their friends and relatives.

23rd of the Month:

Individuals born on the 23rd of themonth have the perfect recipe for success. Such peopleare intelligent, hardworking, well-informed, sensitive, compassionate,understanding, and independent. These individuals are helpful by nature. They are adaptableand like all kinds of challenges. This is the number ofsuccess and money.

24th of the Month:

Individuals born on the 24th of the month are considered very lucky. Such people undergo change very often. They are influential, sincere, helpful, and materially prosperous. They tend to get benefitted from people in powerful positions and are popular.

25th of the Month:

Individuals born on the 25th of the month have this not-so-fortunate combination. The Moon is neutral to Mercury, but Mercury sends out unfriendly vibes toward the Moon. Individuals born on the 25th of the month are sensitive, perceptive, and philosophical and require alone time. They are lucky in love and make substantial financial gains, especially by marriage. Because they are sensitive, when they get upset, they often become distant.They are difficult to become close to,but your friendship with them will continue forever once you become close.

26th of the Month:

Individuals born on the 26th of the month are rigorous, stubborn, and goal-oriented, as it is ruled by Saturn(8). People with this number are advised to select their life partners carefully. They should avoid the bad tendency of being lethargic, sluggish, and fickle-minded. They are skilled at turning a straight forward idea into a profitable venture. For them, "Big is beautiful" fits perfect.

27th of the Month:

Individuals born on the 27th of the month are tenacious, dependable, and passionate. This combination of 2 and 7 gives them initiative and inexhaustible energy. They like diversity and change. Appreciate having responsibilities and having the chance to help others. This combination makes a person commanding and authoritative. These people are both emotional and intuitive.

28th of the Month:

Individuals born on the 28th of the month have to struggle a lot. The native has to face lots of obstacles and opposition. They are successful in the end because of the number 1, a total of 28. They dislike being told what to do and generally find happiness when in charge of their destiny. They are philosophical and spiritual, balancing the material and spiritual world.

29th of the Month:

Individuals born on the 29th of the month naturally experience the energy of the numbers 2 and 9, but they also have the higher potential of the number 11 because $2 + 9 = 11$. It is a compound of uncertainties and insecurities, more influenced by the Moon than Mars. These people achieve success and rise to high positions. With help and cooperation, individuals can make progress. However, their personal life, especially their married life, is not happy.

30th of the Month:

Individuals born on the 30th of the month have a combination of 3(Jupiter) and 0(Infinity) the power of 3 slowed down by 0. Their progress is slow, and they have to work hard to be successful. Thirty folks have to struggle a lot in the first half of their lives. They are thinkers, though, and formulate their own policies. They are sometimes critical by nature. They advocate universal love and brotherhood. Unfortunately, they lack drive and rely more on the charm to get by than on their impressive skills. They achieve the most when working together with someone who frequently encourages them and prods them into action.

31st of the Month:

Individuals born on the 31st of the month have strong managerial and organisational abilities. They typically begin at the bottom of the ladder and advance through the ranks gradually but consistently. They cherish their bonds and are eager to lend a hand to others in need. They leave lasting impressions and never forget a kindness or an offense.

Chapter Three

HISTORY OF LO SHU GRID

"Numerology is the perfect blend of art and science. It taps into the hidden depths of our psyche and brings forth the truths that we may have been hiding from ourselves." - Dan Millman

The Old Chinese philosophers and religious thinkers, in spite of their traditional reverence for the written word, often left ideas unsaid, or only indirectly expressed-either because they and their fellow scholars took them for granted or because the fuller exposition formed part of the esoteric learning that was orally transmitted from teacher to disciple. Some of the key ideas they did not explicitly set down were expressed in various symbols, but, again, they seldom passed on the meanings of these in books, probably for similar reasons. However, an important symbol can sometimes be deciphered by the process of patient analysis, with constant reference to contemporary books and surviving traditions; and, when this is successful, the recovered meanings not only can often serve to supplement the literary texts of that time but may also uncover forgotten traditions, thus giving us new knowledge of the old ideas and beliefs.

A simple diagram from Old China, commonly known as Lo Shu, provides a good example of how well a good symbol reflects the principal idea of its time. It can convey several meanings simultaneously and inspire new ways of thinking.

For over a thousand years, the world of Chinese scholarship has known the Lo Shu as this simple pattern composed of black and white circles or dots arranged in nine groups containing one to nine units each.

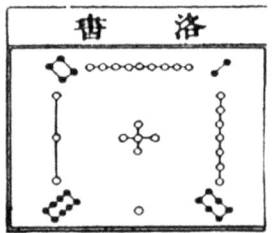

An ancient form of divination, Chinese numerology dates back about 4,000 years. The birth of this art form is retold in the Legend of the Turtle. The mythical Emperor Yu ruled between 2205 and 2198 B.C.E. He had a reputation for being wise and ruling justly. At one time, Emperor Yu was engaged in the supervision of building a dam on the Yellow River. Sitting by the bank of the river, he was interrupted by a divineturtle that appeared from the river. The emperor was astonished when he took acloser look at the back of the Turtle. Therewas a magic square, nine numbers in all. The numbers added up to 15 in every direction.

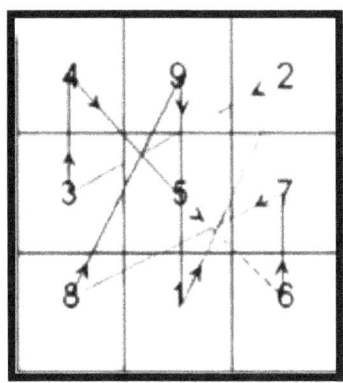

Lo Shu grid is a square-shaped design that consists of 9 numbers from 1 to 9 with three rows and three columns. The total of each row and each column sums to 15. It is considered a sacred square. Chinese numerology has always been associated with the Magical Lo Shu Grid, discovered around 4000 years ago. The intrinsic patterns of the base chart and the way the numbers move about the grid are believed to offer clues on the characteristics and outcomes of events within the environment. The Lo Shu grid is the central principle behind "Flying Star Feng Shui" and is also used to interpret individual birth charts.

In those ancient times in China, it was considered an auspicious omen because they believed that God lived inside tortoise and turtle shells. From this quasi-historical tale, the diagram came to be called the Lo Shu, meaning "Lo River Writing" or "Document of the Lo River" or sometimes simply "Turtle Writing." It was even referred to as the "River Plan." The Lo Shu was also described as "The Celestial Numbers of the Nine Halls." About the beginning of the 2nd century BC, in an early mathematics book by Hsu Yo, a noted astronomer of the Ch'in and Han dynasty, the first reference to the "Nine Halls Calculation" was found in a section on various forms of divination. Again, in the 6th century AD, a commentary by Taoist Chên Luan referred to the Nine Halls by the quotation, 2 and 4 make the shoulders, 6 and 8 make the feet; 3 is at the left, 7 is at the right, 9 is worn on the head, and 1 is underfoot; while five dwells at the center.

The diagram below illustrates the relationship between the eight-sided Pa-Kua and Lo-Shu magic square's nine grids. Please note that the Pa-Kua shown here places the direction of South at the top, to correspond with the number 9. This is because the Chinese compass places South at the top, and to ensure consistency and accuracy, it is necessary when relationships between symbols are being analyzed, and to comply with the practice followed in the ancient manuals.

Pa Kua Image

For practical purposes, however, you may use modern compasses, which place North at the top. However, it is vital that mistakes should not be made while attempting to make an interpretation based on the symbolic relationship between numbers and Trigrams.

The Chinese give equal importance to the Lo-Shu square as they do to the Pa-Kua. It is derived from Laxmi Yantra, similar to the one on the back of the tortoise considered to be the 2nd incarnation of Lord Vishnu. The square is also called a magic square and is believed to give important information while analyzing the building/destiny of the person. Let's look closer at the square and try to see its significance.

4 South East Wood	9 South Fire	2 South West Earth
3 East Wood	5 Centre Earth	7 West Metal
8 North East Earth	1 North Water	6 North West Metal

Chapter Four

MEANING OF NUMBERS AND THEIR ELEMENTARY RELATION

"Numerology is the perfect way to connect with your higher self and understand your spiritual path." - *Unknown*

Numbers	Meanings
1	Communication
2	Sensitivity
3	Imagination
4	Security
5	Balance
6	Support
7	Children
8	Inspiration
9	Humanitarian

This incredible square can help us understand our future. Let's study this as below:

No.s	Direction	Element	Description
1	North	Water	Career, Planning, Initiative
2	Southwest	Earth	Marriage, Happiness
3	East	Wood	Family, Relationships, Growth
4	South East	Wood	Wealth, Prosperity
5	Centre	Earth	Strength, Stability
6	Northwest	Metal	Helpful friend, Friends, Foreign Contracts
7	West	Metal	Mental Peace, Creativity, Children
8	Northeast	Earth	Knowledge, Education, Memory
9	South	Fire	Fame, Energy, Recognition

The Productive Cycle:

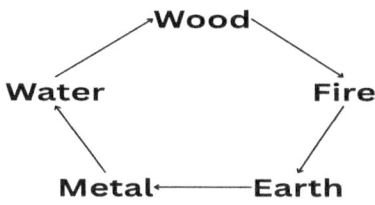

Explaining the Productive Cycle:
- Wood produces Fire: Wood is needed to feed the fire.
- Fire produces Earth: Fire, after burning wood, creates earth in the form of ash.
- Earth produces Metal: Earth is where the metal can be found. Minerals are mined from the soil.
- Metal produces Water: The common explanation is when metal is heated and cooled, water is captured in the air in the form of condensation.
- Water produces Wood: Water is needed for plants to grow.

The Controlling Cycle:

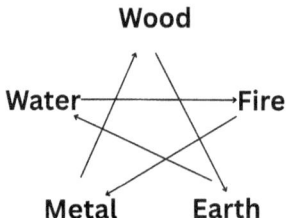

Explaining the Controlling Cycle:
- Fire controls Metal by melting them.
- Metal controls wood: Solid metal can cut down wood.
- Wood controls Earth: Wood depletes nutrients from Earth (the reason why we need fertilizers).
- Earth controls water: Earth controls how water flows (like land formations and dams)
- Water controls fire by extinguishing it.

Chapter Five

HOW TO USE LO SHU GRID

"I can't change the direction of the wind, but I can adjust my sails to always reach my destination." - Jimmy Dean

The Magical Lo Shu grid is divided equally into six parts. Three vertically and three horizontally, respectively. It is also called The LPG (Life Pattern Grid), and there are many ways to look at it. The numbers 4, 9, and 2 in the top row show the head of a person. The middle row, which has the numbers 3, 5, and 7 is the body. The last row, with the numbers 8, 1, and 6 is for the feet.

The top row could be called the **Mental/ Spiritual plane**. It includes thinking, making, imagining, and figuring out. Having to do with Head.
- Ø Sharp brain
- Ø Good memory
- Ø Intellectual skills

Ø Intuitive

The emotional plane is the row in the middle.
Ø spirituality,
Ø Intuition,
Ø Feelings, and emotions.
Ø Also linked to the Torso.

The plane on the bottom row is called **Practical Plane**
Ø ability to do physical work
Ø Creativity
Ø Capacity to be good at sports, have good physical coordination, and be useful in everyday life. To use the head-legs analogy, the feet of the Practical Plane are firmly on the ground.

In the same way, the vertical columns can be understood as follows:

The **Thought plane** is the first of these vertical columns.
Ø This shows how good the person is at coming up with ideas, making things, and seeing them through to the end.
Ø Sharp brain.
Ø Good planning capability
• The **Will plane** is the middle column.
Ø This gives the drive and determination to succeed.
Ø Good will power and self-confidence
Ø Executes the task

The last column on the right is the **Action plane.**
Ø This shows that the person can put his ideas into action.

Ø Good physical energy
Ø Takes quick decisions in life.

The three columns go in a logical order. First, the person needs to think of an idea (Thought plane). He (or she) needs to be determined and keep trying, or the idea will never be put into action. At this point, plans are made. Lastly, the person needs to be able to act on the idea and the desire (Action plane).

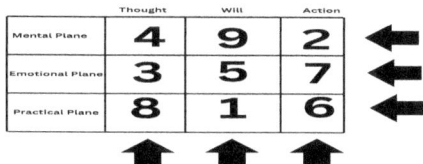

How to use Lo Shu Grid:

Let's take an example to understand how we can use the Lo Shu Grid to understand our life.

How to apply Lo-Shu Grid. Let's take one example of birth date 13th August 1967:

Life purpose number comes to 1+3+8+1+9+6+7 = 35 =3+5 = 8

Place the number of dates of birth and life purpose number in the Lo-Shu square as shown: We also have to add the Kua number, which we will do after the relevant chapter.

This grid is prepared from the full date of birth. The number grid gives 100% vibration and power.

Now, we will create the name grid. For this, I am providing the Chaldean table for easy reference.

Chaldean Numerology

1	2	3	4	5	6	7	8
A	B	C	D	E	U	O	F
I	K	G	M	H	V	Z	P
J	R	L	T	N	W		
Q		S		X			
Y							

This is the Chaldean Numerology chart. Every number has been assigned certain alphabets. This is required to find out the name number.

Let's take the example of Vicky Paul, born on 13thAugust 1967

As per the Chaldean Numerology chart, let us assign numbers to the alphabet.

V I C K Y P A U L

6 1 3 2 1 8 1 6 3

Then fill the grid with each number as many times as it comes in the name. The name grid gives 50% vibrations and power.

Name Grid

Missing	Missing	2
33	Missing	Missing
8	111	66

Number Grid

Missing	9	Missing
3	Missing	7
88	11	6

Now, let's compare both the grids. 4and 5 are missing from both the grids.

2 is missing from the number grid but is present in the name grid. So, she will get the support of number 2 to a certain extent.

Now we can observe that:

A) In the chart, 4 (representing wood element) is missing there by, stability is missing in his life.

How to get cure: Green light in the South- East in the bed room for enhancing consistency.

B) Number 2 (partially) missing & 5 (represent Earth element) is missing there by, whatever he speaks, or acts will not be forceful there by, he is not properly rewarded in life. Not sensitive to other people's feelings. Less intuitive.

Cure: Yellow bulb in the center of the room, and he has to wear a crystal necklace and peaked Himalayan mountain wall poster painting to be put up on the southside corner wall and west side corner wall, there by creating a south west corner with a mountain in his bedroom and office. Keep a green stone pyramid in the south west for strength & stability.

Chapter Six

ARROWS

"Numerology is not just about numbers, it's about energy and how that energy flows through our lives." - Unknown

H*orizontal & Vertical Arrows:*

You should have figured out by now that the rows on the grid are important because they have different numbers. According to Chinese numerology, the following are the meanings of the different arrows.

Most of the arrows in the system were one of two types. The numbers that are there and make a row vertically, horizontally, or diagonally are called "arrows of strengths," while the numbers that aren't there at all in a row vertically, horizontally, or diagonally are called "arrows of weaknesses." Along with these arrows of weaknesses and strengths, we will also see four small arrows in this chapter. These were made by joining the four middle numbers of the outside rows, both horizontal and vertical.

Now, the first thing we do is look at the arrows below.

The Arrows of Strength:

Determination

Emotional

Balance

Spirituality

Intelligence

Prosperity

Capacity to plan

Will power

Action

		2
	5	
8		

The Arrow of Will Power/ Determination:

The numbers 8, 5, and 2 make up this arrow. People who have this arrow are patient, determined, and don't give up easily. They're happy to wait until the right time and then act. They never lose sight of their goals, no matter what happens. Also referred to as Success Plane

2. They are good listeners. Slowly and steadily, they acquire properties.

4		
	5	
		6

The Arrow of Emotional Balance:

This is the number 4, 5, and 6 on the chart. It follows the path of the era of emotional balance. Also, referred to as Success Plane 1. People with this trait are kind, caring, and often make a living by helping other people. They are sensitive and intuitive, and achieve success. These people can seem shy, especially when they are young because they are quiet and gentle.

The Arrow of Wisdom/Intellect (Mental Plane):

In the first row across, the arrow is made up of the numbers 4, 9, and 2. If you have these three numbers, you will be smart and have a good memory. People with this arrow are smart, articulate, and logical, but sometimes they think they are better than other people.

4	9	2

The Spiritual Path of the Arrow (Emotional Plane):

This has the numbers 3, 5, and 7 in it. It is in the middle of the horizontal row. It focuses on how people feel, how they act, and how they are spiritual. It shows that they take life seriously and have an inner calm and peace that don't usually show up before middle age.

3	5	7

The Arrow of Good Fortune (Physical or Practical Plane):

This is in the bottom horizontal row and is made up of the numbers 8, 1 and 6. People who have the arrow of prosperity are very successful in business and commerce. They care about money for its own sake and don't usually care about the more important things in life.

People who have the arrow of prosperity but no numbers on the top horizontal row are cold, calculating, and without emotion. They have a lot of money, but they don't care about how other people feel or what they need.

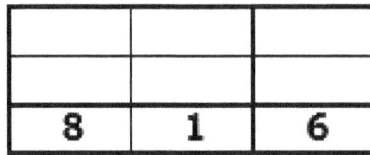

The Planner's Directional Arrow (Thought Plane):

This is the first vertical row of the numbers 4, 3, and 8. This arrow of a planner is a symbol for someone who is smart, sneaky, and not very moral. So, sometimes, whether it's fair or not, it's called the politicians' arrow.

4		
3		
8		

The Arrow of Strength(Will Plane):

This has the numbers 9, 5 and 1 in it. People with this arrow are strong-willed, determined, and don't give up easily. They are often argumentative and have strong feelings about everything. This arrow is seen as a sign of success as people with this arrow keep going until they get where they want to reach.

	9	
	5	
	1	

The Action Arrow (Action Plane):

Action is the keyword for this arrow. It is the last vertical row, which has the numbers 2, 7 and 6. People with this arrow need to have a lot going on and enjoy being active. They like to stay in shape and play sports. They have a lot of energy and are happiest when they can use it to do something physical.

		2
		7
		6

Arrows or Planes with no Numbers on them:

If a plane has all three numbers, the strength of the arrow is 100%.

If a plane has two numbers, the strength of the arrow is 66%.

If the plane has one number present, the strength of the arrow is 33%.

The strength of an arrow that is missing all of its numbers is 0%.

The Arrows of Weakness:

Now we're going to look at the arrows of weakness. **Arrows or planes with no numbers on them**.

Frustration Suspicion Loneliness Apathy Confusion Losses Uncertainty Poor Memory

The Arrow of Frustration (absence of 2, 5, 8):

This arrow indicates that there have been numerous difficulties and set backs. It is viewed as an indication of failure repeatedly. Individuals with this missing arrow should aim to learn from every event and carefully consider their actions before taking action.

The Arrow of Suspicion(absence of 4, 5, 6):

This arrow represents those who are distrustful, cynical, and irritable.

They tend to worry and focus on the unpleasant aspects of life.

This arrow points to a "grey individual."

Indicates a person who lives in perpetual darkness and never sees the light of day.

The Arrow of Loneliness/Skepticism (absence of 3, 5, 7):

This arrow represents a lack of emotion. Individuals with this arrow are so focused on accomplishing their objectives that they neglect their friends and family, and as a result, their lives lack happiness, love, and laughter. People typically suffer from extreme loneliness in their old life. This occurs when 3, 5, and 7 are missing from the grid. They typically hold a conservative view of religion and spirituality. These individuals are caring, trustworthy, and fair, yet they are unable to express themselves. They are born idealistic and highly perceptive.

The Arrow of Apathy(absence of 2, 6, 7):

This arrow is generated when the last vertical row of the chart is missing the numbers 2, 6, and 7. Those afflicted with apathy lack drive and fail to seize opportunities knocking at their door. These individuals are indecisive, fearful of taking risks, and have generally accomplished only a fraction of what they could if they exerted more effort.

The Arrow of Confusion (absence of 4, 3, 8):

This missing arrow shows up because there are no 8, 3, or 4 in the chart. It is in the left most vertical column. People who have this arrow are not logical, organized, or methodical. They don't make plans for more than a few days ahead and then self-sabotage their own plans.

The Arrow of Losses(absence of 8, 1, 6):

This arrow is made when the numbers 8, 1, and 6 are not in the bottom row. So, this Arrow hasn't been on anyone's charts in the 20th century, but it will be back in the 21st century. People like these will try to make money by taking part in easy get-rich schemes. They will always fail at these things, and they won't realize it until they are middle-aged. If they had put the same amount of work into a single worth while goal, they would have been successful.

The Arrow of Uncertainty/Indecision (9, 5, 1):

This is because the numbers 1, 5 and 9 are not in the middle vertical row. No one has this arrow born in the 1900s. Now, many people will be having this missing arrow of weakness.

People with this arrow really want to be liked and accepted. So, it's easy for others to lead and change them. They will have a hard time standing up for what they believe in because they want everyone to like them and can't say things that other people might not agree with.

The Arrow of Poor Memory (absence of 2, 4, 9):

The lack of the numbers 4, 9 and 2 in the top horizontal row results in the arrow. The 31st century will be the time when this arrow will appear again. In their birth chart, everyone born in the previous century had a 9 and everyone born in the following century will have a 2.

This arrow indicates that an individual's intellectual capacity is robust early in life but gradually declines as they get older. These folks can have mental instability and are regularly overcome by the intensity of their ideas.

Small Arrows:
- Detail and Deceit
- Litigation
- Peace of Mind
- Science

The four middle numbers of the outside horizontal and vertical rows are joined to form these four little arrows. These tiny arrows connect the numbers 1 and 3, 3 and 9, 9 and 7, and 7 and 1, respectively.

The Hint of Deception and Detail (1, 3):

When both a 1 and a 3 are present on the chart, this row is produced. This combination makes people detail-oriented. In fact, if any number appears more than once, the individual has a tendency towards perfectionism. The arrow also has a negative aspect. In an effort to safeguard themselves, they might fabricate information or hide the facts.

The Litigation Arrow (3, 9):

When the chart has both the 3 and 9 numbers, this arrow is produced. This combination makes people more likely to debate and get embroiled in conflicts of all types. This combination is known as the arrow of litigation because if these issues become too serious, they must be resolved in court.

The Peace of Mind Arrow (7, 9):

People with this combination are optimistic, self-assured, and have a firm faith. The arrow is formed when the chart contains both a 9 and a

7. The spirituality of the 7 benefits from the rationality of the 9, and vice versa. This constituency is capable of responding to various circumstances with composure and faith that things will turn out for the best.

The Arrow of Science(1, 7):

Individuals whose birth charts include the numbers 1 and 7 are curious about the wonders of our universe. They adore looking for the hidden facts and can get bogged down in their research if they let it. Often, they have an interest in the sciences (frequently those that concern the oceans).

Chapter Seven

REPETITIVE NUMBERS

"You have to be odd to be number one." – *Anonymous*

The following is the table of the key words, which interprets what it means when a particular number comes in the grid more than once.

Number	Once	Twice	Thrice	Four times
1	Introvert	Communicative	Talkative	Compassionate
2	Sensitive	Bright	Very sensitive	Loners
3	Excellent	Creative	Over imaginative	Over imaginative
4	Orderly/ stable	Pragmatic	Hard working	Physically more active
5	Caring	Persistent	Determined	Impulsive
6	Good advisers	Original	High tempered	Emotional
7	Learn through experience	Spiritual	Learn through loss	Difficulties in many areas of life
8	Scrupulous	Adamant	Materialistic	Ceaselessly in motion
9	Intelligent	Critical	Givers	Brilliant and loners

Here are the numbers, their frequency, and their meaning in more detail:

NUMBER 1:

- Once: They find it difficult to communicate their deepest feelings.
- Twice: They can communicate effectively and comprehend other people's view points. They have a fair-minded and impartial perspective on life.
- Three Times: They can talk endlessly and then exhibit silence and lack of communication. Each of these characteristics are frequently seen in cheerful, talented, outgoing, and entertaining people.
- Four Times: They have trouble relaxing. Most of the time, they are hyper. If the name has four 1s, people will frequently misunderstand them despite being sensitive and caring. Clear speech could also be challenging.
- Five Times: They are most ill at ease speaking in front of a sizable audience. They do, however, make fantastic authors, painters, or dancers, with a propensity to indulge excessively in wine, food, and lovers.

NUMBER 2:

- Once: They are sensitive and easily hurt by others' words or actions. They can spot devious people right away. If you have a single 2, you are intelligent and sensitive. Working in a calm environment is preferable to doing so in a competitive one. You can learn a lot about a person at just a single glance.
- Two Times: They are exceptionally intelligent and perceptive, which makes them good psychics.

- Three Times: Those with three 2s in their birth date are intuitive and sensitive but prone to getting hurt easily. You might be talented in music as well.
- Four Times: Such people can be tough to manage because they can be extremely irritable and picky. They are considered eccentric and often prefer to be alone. They could over react to people and circumstances when made to wait.
- Five Times: They are born whiners and complainers.

It will never be easy to trust others if born with five 2s. They will suffer if they don't have confidence in and trust in themselves.

NUMBER 3:
- Once: They have a sharp memory and a distinct understanding of their objectives. They are capable and born to lead.
- Two Times: They have excellent emotive skills and are very imaginative.

Two 3s indicate intelligence and creativity. Many authors belong to this category. Such people are given to day dreaming. It is also evident that getting the creative juices flowing is vital.

- Three Times: They are highly imaginative, living in their own universe, and it becomes difficult for them to relate with the outer world. They have a habit of day dreaming.
- Four Times: Due to their vivid imagination, they could appear paranoid.

It can be challenging to manage daily life if you have four 3s in the chart, as this can make you incredibly imaginative and impractical.

NUMBER 4:
- Once: They keep their surroundings clean and orderly and work systemically. They might have musical talent.
- Twice: They have a strong materialistic attitude. They are incredibly artistic and creative people who enjoy doing their work.
- Three Times: Although they work hard and are physically fit, their energies are typically channeled in the wrong direction.

Such people are responsible, well- organized, and diligent if they have three 4s. Nonetheless, they could frequently disregard everything else for their work and the material world. They can also make poor selections at work.

- Four Times: They are skilled workers, particularly in manual labor. They put in the arduous effort and favor vocations requiring physical labor. The cerebral or spiritual is hard to comprehend.

NUMBER 5:
- Once: They require a lot of flexibility in their personal or professional interactions. They can not be bound. Having a healthy sense of balance, they are very sympathetic, proactive, and skilled at inspiring others. They are effective leaders.
- Twice: They are tenacious and diligent. They have a lot of energy, drive, and determination, though a false sense of self-assurance could trip them up. They must learn to control their emotional outbursts because that frequently lead to issues at home. They might abuse alcohol, drugs, or excessive sex.
- Three Times: They are habitual talkers who do not pause to consider their words. Usually, they immediately regret

what they said. They are bold, do unconventional things, and visit unusual locations.

- Four Times: They frequently get into accidents or even start them. They develop impulsivity and stop deliberating before acting.

NUMBER 6:

- Once: They value maintaining a comfortable environment and are devoted to their family. They are terrific listeners and advisors. Typically, people ask for their opinion.
- Twice: They are inventive but also authoritarian parents that worry constantly and without valid cause. If you have two 6s in your graph, you tend to be too protective, especially around kids. You love to be around beautiful things because you are creative and know what looks good.

Such people often have artistic or musical skills. Even though they are creative, they don't believe in their own skills. They can only be successful if their friends and family back them up and cheer them on. They tend to worry about their home and family all the time. After small set backs, they take a long time to get back on their feet.

- Three Times: They have an extremely volatile personality. They have bad tempers and need to learn to control them. They need to channel their creativity, which helps them excel in their chosen vocations.
- Four Times: They were outcasts as kids due to their tremendous creativity and emotion. They enjoy tantrums, but if given the right instruction when young, they develop into experts in their chosen subjects.

NUMBER 7:
- Once: They will learn a lesson by after losing something important to them, whether it be a person or an item, and in turn, it might turn their attention to spirituality and metaphysics. A single 7, without a 3 or 5, will make them want to find hidden truths and strive for perfection.
- Twice: They express curiosity about the after life and the spiritual realm. Their ability to think logically qualifies them to solve technical problems.
- Three Times: They frequently experience fraud, dishonesty, and money losses throughout their unhappy lives. But because of their resilient inner selves, they are able to bear everything.
- Four Times: They experience all of life's issues with regard to their health, home, and finances.

NUMBER 8:
- Once: They pay attention to detail and are reliable. They enjoy variety and have busy minds. They dislike performing mundane tasks.
- Twice: They are incisive and meticulous. They are more active than passive. Once they've made a decision, they don't change it.
- Three Times: They are extremely hedonistic and materialistic. They are great entrepreneurs who only want the best for themselves and enjoy all the comforts money can buy.
- Four Times: They require change frequently and are quite restless. They are frequently either in jail or on the road.

NUMBER 9:
- Once: They are intelligent enough to distinguish right from wrong. It indicates intellectual learning.
- Twice: They have an intellectual bent and are judgmental of others because they believe they are the only ones with superior intelligence.
- Three Times: They are kind and idealistic. They frequently like to exaggerate circumstances. They have a lot of mental energy with the three 9s. But, if things don't go according to plan, they may feel horrible.
- Four Times: They are extremely clever while being loners or living in their own world. They can positively impact our society and make excellent leaders if their energies and intelligence are appropriately channeled.

Arguments with their partner are likely to ensue when the number 9 repeatedly appears in their life. The issue is that they ignore their heart and simply pay attention to their thoughts. Even if they are polite and tactful, they risk becoming overly idealistic. They might be reserved and aloof when it comes to love.

Chapter Eight

MISSING NUMBERS

"There is strength in numbers, but organizing those numbers is one of the great challenges."
- John C. Mather

M*issing Number 1:*
- Difficulty in expressing their inner views
- As always need support from others
- Little or no ego
- May stammer at an earlyage

Missing Number 2:
- Lack of sensitivity and intuition. May not care for others' feelings
- Will not admit their mistakes and try to justify their actions.

Missing Number 3:
- Lack of creativit
- Poor imagination power
- May submit to difficulties.

Missing Number 4:

- Lack of discipline and organization
- Clumsy hands

Missing Number 5:
- Lack of balance in every sphere of life
- Lack of drive or versatility to achieve their goals

Missing Number 6:
- Poor bonding with home and famil
- Weak relationship sector
- May face marriage problem
- Will not get support from society at the time of crunch

Missing Number 7:
- Lack of spirituality, religion, occult, education
- May not care for the feelings of others

Missing Number 8:
- Poor in financial management
- Spend thrift

Missing Number 9:
- Over look the feelings of others, lack of intelligence, energy
- May not care for others' feelings.

Missing Numbers in Detail:

Number 1:

People who don't have the number one will find it hard to show who they are and what makes them special. They will probably not have any issues with ego and pride, and they'll probably spend most of their time helping and supporting other people. People who are lazy or afraid may be unable to set career goals or miss opportunities when planning their careers.

Their careers sometimes get in the way,and they can't take a different path.

Number 2:

If the native doesn't have Number 2, they aren't sensitive or intuitive enough. People like this are also very impatient and unreliable in their day-to-day jobs. They may also be too worried about explaining and justifying their actions, or lack there of. Because they don't listen to their guts, they make mistakes.

Number 3:

People who lack self-confidence and find it hard to talk about themselves in most situations may miss a number 3. They tend to underrate their skills, which makes them more likely to doubt themselves. Also, these people can't think clearly when they face distractions and failures and can't get ahead in life without the help of mentors who are at a higher level. This can continue for the initialyears of their lives and become better once they learn to accept themselves for what they truly are. Once that happens, they will gain confidence, self-belief, and esteemfrom all their endeavors. Till then, they tend to underrate theirskills, which makes them more likely to doubt themselves.

Number 4:

Those who don't have number 4 in their chart aren't organized, which is the most important skill they should work on. Working in set routines, with set norms, becomes a big issue for them. They are also prone to arriving late. They also don't have much self-motivation or patience, and they can't deal with small problems. If they lack consistency or drive, they may make hasty decisions that will cost them money. Life will improve once they acquire a passion for their wants and more tolerance and patience toward others.

Number 5:

Those who don't have number 5 will find setting clear and targeted goals a big problem. They don't have any drive or desire. They aren'tvery good at doing more than one thing at once,so they need help from outside sources to stay on track. Also, these people need help setting goals and objectives that are realistic. Nature won't make life stable and balanced.

Number 6:

People whose charts/grids are missing the number 6 are more likely to keep their deepest feelings to themselves. Even with the people they care about the most, they are not selfless. Because of this, they find it hard toget along with others and may even have trouble with strangers. They may also not have enough money, joy, or luxury.

Number 7:

When number 7 is missing, a person is careless, doesn't care about how others feel, and lives for themselves. In their daily lives, they are often disorganized and tend to stay away from others. They hate being left alone. They stay away from everything spiritual or meta physical.

Number 8:

A person missing number eight may not know how to work in the real world. People who don't have this number have trouble keeping track of their money and are generally bad at handling their financial affairs. Also, they don't have ambition or drive and don't do all of their daily chores because they are careless and don't take their work seriously.

Number 9:

Everyone from the 20th century has this number, but in the 21st century, many people will not have 9 in their charts. People like this are often insensitive and don't care about what other people need. People who are cold and rude to others must learn to care about others.They need to cultivate that much-required streak of humanitarianism. They don't have a name or fame in society, aren't appreciated by society, and have low self-esteem.

Chapter Nine

ANALYZING TWO LO SHU GRIDS FOR COMPATIBILITY

"Numbers are not merely symbols—they are the key to understanding human nature, relationships, and destiny." — Cheiro (William John Warner)

To evaluate compatibility, you simply place the two 3×3 charts next to each other for

a direct comparison.

Essential highlights are:

Numbers that align perfectly: When both partners share identical numbers, they effortlessly harmonize in that area. For example, when both partners carry a 6, it indicates a shared commitment to family and domestic values, which is often regarded as essential for a successful marriage.

Numerology studies frequently highlights that common core numbers, particularly 2, 4, or 6, indicate a sense of alignment. When one partner possesses a certain quality or trait while the other lacks it, the partner with that quality can effectively bridge the gap for their counterpart. If Partner A is missing a 2 (relationship focus) while Partner B possesses 2, B's strength can effectively offset A's deficiency.

Conversely, if one individual possesses multiple instances of a number that the other lacks entirely, this discrepancy may necessitate attention. One can suggest that when one partner lacks certain numbers while the other has an abundance, it may indicate an imbalance that necessitates intentional communication and mutual understanding.

A particular number is absent in both the partners: If neither partner possesses a number, that characteristic is lacking in the relationship. The absence of 7 in both the charts indicates a shared deficiency in spiritual focus or introspection that may require nurturing. Typically, any missing number indicates a shortfall in one or both charts, meaning that shared absent numbers underscore common challenges. Additionally, you have the option to compare active "planes" (rows/columns). If both partners possess all three numbers in the top row (4-9-2), it indicates that they both have robust mental faculties and intellect. Complementary plane alignments, such as both featuring the middle column 9-5-1 in action, indicate a synergy of willpower. When planes are misaligned, they often reveal varying life priorities. Numerology guides often discuss the significance of aligning vertical or diagonal "energy paths," such as both partners possessing the 2-5-8 diagonal, indicating a shared direction.

Number Pairings: Compatible vs. Incompatible

According to the Lo Shu tradition, specific numbers are believed to either harmonize or clash in terms of energy. Although interpretations differ, here are some popular pairings to consider:

1 and 3 are a perfect match: Leadership and initiative frequently complement creativity and communication effectively. They have the ability to inspire one another's creativity.

On the other hand, 1 & 6 (not compatible): The confrontation between Water (1) and Metal (6) is perceived as a battle. "1 typically works well with 3, but there may be some conflicts with 6.

Earth trio: 2, 5, 8 (compatible) Each of the three embodies the essence of the Earth element. Individuals with 2, 5, and 8 in their charts often experience a sense of stability when they come together. For instance, 2 embodies partnership energy, 8 signifies ambition, and 5 represents flexibility – creating a harmonious blend.

1 (Water) & 9 (Fire) (incompatible): In the realm of Chinese elements, water puts out fire. A person who excels in one area may inadvertently stifle a partner's strengths, leading to tension. According to another guide, 1 is associated with Water (North direction) while 9 represents Fire (South) – a naturally opposing pair.

6 (Metal) & 9 (Fire) (incompatible): The relationship between metal and fire is one of control, as fire has the power to melt metal. A 6, representing a metal element, paired with a 9, embodying a fire element, may face challenges due to their inherently conflicting natures.

Matching duals: Certain sources highlight that aligning "core numbers" such as 2-4-6 across both charts creates a sense of harmony. For example, when two individuals possess robust 6's (love/family), they frequently discover that domestic life comes effortlessly to them.

In the end, these combinations serve as merely suggestions rather than rigid guidelines. They direct the pathways of harmonious energy (similar or complementary elements) and highlight potential friction points (conflicting energies).

Let us take example grids.

Male Date of Birth: 28/07/1966. Destiny Number: 3

Female Date of Birth: 27/05/1969. Destiny Number: 3

	9	2
3		7
8	1	66

28/07/1966

	99	2
3	5	7
	1	6

27/05/1969

In this example, the male native isproviding the energy of 8 to the female native. She is providing the energy ofmissing 5 in the male chart. And none of them have number 4. In such situations remedy becomes essential.

Chapter Ten

PERSONAL YEARS

"When we use numerology to decipher the meaning of the numbers and apply them to ourselves, we discover the secrets of who we are." - *Anonymous*

Every year, we and our world go through different sets of conditions known as the "personal" and "universal" year cycles. Universal cycles are very easy to determine. Simply, add up the numbers of the year, be it past or present, to know the numeric influence of that year. Let's take a year in the past, 1990. It adds up to a 1 (1+9+9+0=19;1+9=10; 1). This year has an energy of 1 and will affect all of us. Now, let's take a year in the future, 2030.

It adds up to 5 (2+0+3+0=5). 2030 will have the universal energy of 5, affecting all of us.

The personal year cycle, however, affects us in a more personal way. To find the personal year number of an individual, take the birth date, birth month and add to that particular year. This can be done for any year an individual wants to know. Take the example of 27th May. I add it to the present year of

2023. 2+7+5+2+0+2+3=21=2+1=3. The personal year of this individual in 2023 is 3. This year will vibrate with number 3 energies.

Personal Year 1:

THEME: Sowing Seeds, Rebirth, and the Start of an Era.

This marks the start of a fresh nine-year cycle. What has worried you for the past years is now completely unimportant, and you might even discover that your priorities have shifted completely. Simply put, past disappointments don't matter any more. Any work you do during this year establishes the tone and framework for the following nine. Decide on your goals now and take action towards them. A personal year one frequently results in renewed vitality and physical vigor.

Number 1 will rule over you this year. Challenges and issues that have persisted for along time will be lessened during this time. One will be fortunate and receive assistance from many individuals, especially officials and people in positions of influence.

This year one will: Feel physically and mentally healthier and more progress-oriented

- If a person is organized and makes preparations in advance, they can succeed in their jobs and businesses.
- Make a significant adjustment in your life; all changes should be made to improve your living circumstances.
- Make new friends who will be valuable in the future.
- Continue to be fearless and worry-free.
- Work hard while being less stressed.
- Get fame and popularity.

Also, this year is good for reading, writing, and launching a new business.

Personal Year 2:

THEME: Waiting for the ideal moment, nurturing, harmony and development.

This is when the seeds of change you sowed in a year-one cycle begin to sprout. Year 2 is all about endurance. You should use this year to meet new friends and allies and make any necessary adjustments to your personal life that might be getting in the way of your success.

This year is often regarded as the most difficult because it is frequently fraught with difficulties and delays, but in the end, any difficulties you face will only sharpen your best traits.

This year, you will be controlled by the following factors:

- A rise in one's own magnetism
- New acquaintances who will prove useful in the future.
- Reduced anxiety and tension
- Pragmatism to overcome emotional turbulence.
- Benefits from real estate.
- A new home or apartment
- A shift in perspective.
- Better living conditions thanks to persistence and careful preparation.

One should try to stay away from needless anxiety and haste this year.

Personal Year 3:

THEME: Growth, Personal and Business Success, and Blossoming

This is a very joyful year in which you start to realise the results of your labors. You might anticipate pleasant surprises and fulfilment in various spheres of your life, including business, work, friends, and love. You have such a zest for life that people can find it hard to resist you. You typically discover that your responsibility load is some how reduced during the third year. The only negative aspect of this year is that there are so many wonderful chances available to you that you might be tempted to take on more than you can handle.

This year also brings

- Greater information and sensible experience
- Time to finish off unfinished tasks;
- Making new friends and acquaintances
- Prosperity, fame, fortune, and honor. It helps one communicate their ideas more clearly. It has particular significance for authors, lecturers, and orators. In their public speaking or writing, these persons need to exercise caution. They may become more forthright and bold under Jupiter's influence.
- Beneficial for launching a new business or endeavor.
- Helpful in organizing and finishing tasks.
- A year for receiving a promotion at work.
- A period when one should not blindly trust friends

Personal Year 4:

THEME: Upkeep, labor, restraint, and responsibility

You will be working really hard and exercising discipline during this year as you try to fulfil all the commitments you made during year 3. A lot of people find year four to be very frustrating as their responsibilities grow. "One step forward, two steps back" is a typical metaphor used to represent this year.

Although it may feel like you are not making much progress, the purpose of year four is to lay a solid foundation that will allow your life goals to mature over the following two years.

This year will bring:
- Success despite challenges
- Stability, unaffected by unforeseen problems and challenges.
- Vigilance, diligence, and composure
- Increased income streams, financial stability, and improvements in wealth.
- New endeavors, including moving into a new home or apartment.

Other possibilities for this year:
- A marriage is auspicious.
- Beneficial for friendships and romantic partnerships.
- Ineffective for romantic relationships.
- Beneficial for interactions with officials and other powerful individuals.

Excellent for religious and spiritual activity as well as travel.

Personal Year 5:

THEME: Independence, freedom, and interpersonal connections, travel.

This year, there may be numerous favorable prospects. Several of the challenges from prior years seem to be disappearing. More personal freedom and a break from stifling routines are the rewards for your hard work.

The big picture may include travel, adventure, or further education. This year is also beneficial for seeking out new careers or for socializing. Alternately, you might move. The fact that you might feel like working less or have a tendency to avoid responsibility is a downside of this year.

- It's a year of achievement and financial security that widens one's social network.
- Beneficial to company and business people.
- Ideal for travel and trips abroad for pleasure or business.
- Beneficial for business partnerships.
- Be mindful when concluding an agreement or contract
- Beneficial for people working in the media and communications industry, including journalists, authors, poets, actors, and entertainers.

Personal Year 6:

THEME: Responsibility, love, family, and a home.

A personal year 6 makes it easier to form new emotional connections and amplifies feelings in current ones. During this stage, a lot of people meet their soul partners. During this blissful year, you're most likely to get married or become engaged. This can be a lovely experience, but it can also be humbling because it frequently forces people to choose whether to commit or not. Also, you might choose to spend more time with close friends or family. A friend you make throughout this cycle is probably going to stick with you forever.

- Beneficial for family relationships; unencumbered by home life concerns; favorable for romance and conceiving.
- Beneficial for individuals working in the entertainment industry, including film makers, actors, musicians, poets, painters, interior decorators, and musicians. Excellent for spending on decorating, entertainment, and pleasure.
- Good for people in the jewelry and perfume industries.

- A chance for unemployed people to find work.
- A time to deal with gifts, sensuous objects, worldly pleasures, and beautiful things. This year, the possibility of gaining unanticipated cash and a pay increase is also present.

Personal Year 7:

THEME: Self-analysis, learning, and self discovery

Even if you have a reputation for being an extrovert, a year seven will probably make you want to be alone. You might want to pursue your interests, go on a trip, or find a method to escape work demands. Year seven is similar to the psyche's cocooning stage, when you evaluate, contemplate, and work to shed any habits, connections, or patterns that might impede your personal development. Also, this year is favorable for any type of self-improvement, including medical procedures, counseling, therapy, and higher education.

- Problems and misunderstandings.
- Business difficulties. More work and less money.
- Accomplishment in activities like lawsuits and judicial proceedings.

The year will also serve as a test for your friends and helpers.

- Focus your efforts on astrology, Tantra magic, hypnosis, and the healing arts.
- Be more conservative.
- Be careful when having romantic relationships because there is a danger of gaining a poor reputation.
- Be upbeat and unperturbed if you want to succeed in the tasks you embark on. Problems and hurdles can be overcome with persistence and optimism. The challenges are merely a test.

The year will also be fruitful for people who practice healing, astrology, and esoteric sciences.

Personal Year 8:

THEME: Achievement, Career, Power, Wealth, and Abundance

This is a powerful year that often boosts all areas of your life significantly, but it especially benefits your profession and financial situation. This year is a wonderful time to purchase a new home, look for employment, or implement a business strategy. While you're in the eighth year, people find you more alluring and captivating, and many people find themselves suddenly catapulted into positions of enormous authority or power. During this lucrative cycle, if you put your attention on making money, you'll probably succeed.

This year will be:

- Beneficial for social workers, legislators, and those working in the iron and steel sector. It provides the chance to launch a new business.

- Not good in terms of health. There must be precautions. Avoid tension, excitement, and fear. Increase your intake of juices and spices to strengthen your heart and detoxify your blood.

- A time to succeed in material pursuits; one should channel their attention into developing their creative faculties. Energy used properly will result in luck.

- Effective for winning court cases and battles with adversaries.

- An opportunity to develop independence and rely on one's own judgement and resources.

- Beneficial for social work.

Personal Year 9:

THEME: Endings, completions, dreams fulfilled and the end of an era.

The year nine symbolizes completion and the end of everything you were able to accomplish in the previous ten years. Many people find that this year is uncomfortable, especially if they are resistant to change. Something that used to intrigue you may no longer do so, and you may experience restlessness. If you are unable to do so voluntarily, a circumstance may arise that compels you to make a change. You will get what you sow this year.

The number nine (9) will bring

- A successful and prosperous year.
- A period when desires can be satisfied.
- A period for self-organization.
- A year of getting special treatment from powerful men and elected leaders.

It will also result in

- Little disputes that could lead to an officer and you exchanging hurtful exchanges.
- Victory in battle and in completions.
- Respect from society.
- The potential for unforeseen financial advantages due to a lottery win, an inheritance, or some other circumstance.

Also, one should stay away from perfectionism and doubt this year. The year will be fruitful if more effort is put into spiritual activities.

Chapter Eleven

SOME OTHER IMPORTANT NUMBERS HOUSE, VEHICLE, & MOBILE

"Numerology is not just about numbers, it's about energy and how that energy flows through our lives." - Unknown

***H**ouse Numbers:*

The number of your house or apartment is also very important as it is literally where you live. Add the digits of the house number until it is reduced to a single digit. Do not include the block or building number as it is common to all the people living there. But, if there is any alphabet attached with your number then turn the letters into numbers and come to your house number.

House No. 1:

Encourages being independent, creative, ambitious, driven, and a leader. If you are self- employed and work from home, this is a great place to live. This is also a great home for people who want to live together but still have their own space and freedom. Living here can make you stronger, more determined, and more sure of yourself. Do not try too hard to make every one in the family to mingle. Every inhabitant of this house will require space for himself or herself.

House No. 2:

This home will always be a warm, loving place where people feel welcome, cared for, and loved. The energy of the number 2 is soft and emotional. So, this is a great place for people who like to be surrounded by pictures of their family and friends and who like to have small, close-knit gatherings where feelings are shared and love is shown. It's a great place for couples who like to do things together. It works best for people who are in a relationship, friends, and young couples and families. This home is also good for writers and healers because the 2 energy encourages intuition and balance. Do not clutter this house. Clutter will make people irritable. This house number functions well when everything is at its place and in harmony.

House No. 3:

This house is sure to feel happy and positive. Three is a fun and lively number, so this is a great place to get together with friends and have a good time. It has a very creative vibe, so if you want to start a family or a creative project, this is a great place to do so. Here, people talk openly about how they feel, and they also share new and interesting ideas. This is a great home for artists, singles, couples, or families who love to live life to the fullest and express themselves with joy. Do not be very serious or tidy in this house or else it will stifle the light hearted atmosphere of the house.

House No. 4:

This is a safe, solid, and protected place. The number 4 is the most rooted of all the numbers. It has to do with the earth, real estate, and physical structures. This would be a great place to put your money into real estate, stocks, money, or even your education. Here, there is support for discipline, structure, and taking responsibility. This is a great place to live if you want to grow your business, your money, or your family. It is also a place to live if you like things to stay the same or if you want a normal home even if the rest of your life is exciting! Avoid leaving any maintenance and gardening unfinished. Do not be disorganized in this house.

House No. 5:

If you like to meet new people, this is the place to be. 5 loves to party, so there's never a dull moment. The number 5 is the friendliest of all the numbers, so this is a great place for people who like to have people over and keep them entertained. Children thrive here, and so do pets. With 5, there are always surprises, so if you like excitement and new experiences, you've come to the right place. Perfect for people who like to travel, meet new people, try new things, and enjoy their freedom. You've come to the right place if you want to change up your routine, get out of a rut, or just have fun! Do not try to make this place a quiet one. If you want solitude go to a park or for a walk.

House No. 6:

This home will bring beauty, love, and harmony to a family, a couple, or an artist. Your home really is your safe place. When people walk into your home, they will feel right at home because the energy is balanced. It's nice to be surrounded by art and beauty, so you'd want to fill your home with pretty colors, comfy furniture, and plants. You will want to help and care for other people, so children and animals do well here. A 6 home can make almost any kind of person happy. You're very fortunate to live here. Keep this house well decorated. Also, do not neglect things made by children as this is very important for this house.

House No. 7:

You will love living here if you area mystic, writer, researcher, or spiritual seeker of any kind. 7 is a private and sometimes secretive vibration. It makes you think, reflect, and get powerful new ideas. You will do well here if you like to come home and have quiet time to read, think, and rest. If you don't already live near water, water is a beautiful thing to add to this home to make it more peaceful. You can have some exciting spiritual and intellectual realizations here, so it's a great place to live if you want to make big changes in your consciousness. Do not try to host a "party of the year" in this house as it will be a flop. No gaudy colours or loud music in this house.

House No. 8:

This is the place to be if you want to start your own business or move up in your job. Even better if you can run your business from home. 8 is a number of wealth and plenty, so anything to do with money will do well here. 8 is also the number of passions, so you will be encouraged to spend time with people and activities you care deeply about. Strength-based physical activities will get a boost. This is a great place to live if you want to grow your status in the world, your position in life, your wealth, or the size of your family. Do not hang heavy curtains and do not let the upkeep of the house go sideways.

House No. 9:

In a 9 home, everyone is welcome. 9 makes people feel like they are loved and accepted. This is the number of love and kindness for everyone. Your sense of what's right will be at its best. You might get phone calls and visits from people who want your advice. People will want to come to your home because it has a loving vibe. Since 9 is an international number, you may want to travel, or welcome visitors from far off places. Don't run a business from this house unless it is of a charitable nature.

Relevance of your Vehicle Number:

One of the most important numbers in your life is the number on your car. It has to do with how you travel, what kind of travel you do, and how safe your travel is. No number is "bad," so there's no reason to worry. But it's good to know how well your vehicle number matches up with your own numbers, especially your personality and life path numbers, because when we drive, we revert to a more instinctual self.

Let us use MH 43 BE 5682 as an example.

First, there is the number as a whole. We get this number by adding up the digits and the letter values that go with them.

4+5+4+3+2+5+5+6+8+2=44=8

The second is the sum of the numbers unique to the person

5+6+8+2=21=3

Third is the sum of the letters: 4+5+2+5=16=7

The numbers stand out the most and show how people see you. The total of the letters tells you about the purpose and type of trip, while the overall numbers tells you about the vehicle. If you aren't compatible with these numbers, you may have trouble getting where you want to go in life. People are slowly learning how important it is to buy their own personalized number plate because of this.

MH 43 BE is common to many. 5682 is unique to the person in the example taken. Ideal case should be that the unique and common numbers combined should be friendly to you.

Practically, at least the unique total should be friendly.

Number 1: Very single minded driver. Always on the move and a good driver.

Number 2: This number makes you think a little too much about other drivers. A considerate driver.

Number 3: You like to drive. You might go out a lot to have fun. The car can be personalized and flashy.

Number 4: You may have a car that is well taken care of. You care about how things work. Don't worry too much about how clean the car is.

Number 5: The temptation here is to multitask while you drive. Make sure that you have a hands free mobile.

Number 6: Very good for a family car, for going on outings and everything to do with community work.

Number 7: You tend to go into a world of your own. Must be mindful while driving.

Number 8: Be calm while you drive and get a hands free set. You love driving an impressive set of wheels.

Number 9: Giving lifts and carpooling will make it worthwhile. This vehicle needs to be environment friendly.

Relevance of your Mobile Numbers:

Another very important number in our life is our mobile number. It can also be called our identity as we are giving out our numbers to people, all the time. We are in touch with the outside world through our mobile phones. If our birth number or destiny number is not in harmony with our mobile number, or we are not getting enough calls we would like to get, it could be worth changing the same, to get the desired results.

Any number which is associated with you for a very long time impacts us, colors our life. Be it house number or mobile number or landline number. You arrive at it the same way as all other numbers - by adding all the digits and reducing it to a single number. However, notice the individual digits also because if one or two of them repeats several times it can impact the final number. It is always better to prepare a mobile number grid, along with date of birth grid, and name grid. And, then compare all three grids.

Mobile Number 1:

You are left to your own devices most of the time. This number is not ideal for chatting, relaxed, frank and social communications.

Mobile Number 2:

You will probably be called to ask for advice most of the times. People will look up to you as the one to sort their issues. Expect heart to heart chat on this number.

Mobile Number 3:

This is a good number for sales and anything and everything creative. Light banter and jokes comes easy. Lots of fun but not much work gets done.

Mobile Number 4:

Practical solutions are the key. Always say what you mean and stick to your commitments. No chit chat on this number.

Mobile Number 5:

This is an impatient number. If not careful chances of arguments are there. Ideas are overflowing so keep notepad and pen handy before the ideas desert you. Good number for journalism and to keep a big contact list.

Mobile Number 6:

Good number for creativity. Doing community work. You may be tempted to call home a lot.

Mobile Number 7:

This is a quiet number. You may not feel like answering calls on this number. Chances of misunderstandings are quite possible. You may get strong intuitions while on a call with this number.

Mobile Number 8:

This is a boss number. You come across as quite authoritative. Be firm, but also be polite.

Mobile Number 9:

A chat can very easily turn into a spiritual or philosophical discussion. Great number for arranging trips and holidays.

Chapter Twelve

KUA NUMBER

"Feng Shui is the perfect tool for breaking vicious circles." - Stefan Edmunds

In Feng Shui, Kua Number is an important idea. In Lo Shu also it is used extensively to find out about our lucky directions. The Date of Birth and Gender of a person are used to figure out their Kua number. Feng Shui says that a person's birth year has an effect on some of their qualities, skills, and other traits. It's also known as the Eight Mansions or Eight Houses of Feng Shui. Your Kua Number may also be called your bagua number, or personal trigram.

What is My Kua Number?

Once you know your Kua number, it's easy to find the best compass directions for your work, love, health, wealth, and other parts of your life. Four of the eight mansions (the eight compass directions) will be good luck, and four will be bad luck. With this information, you can improve all parts of your life and stay away from directions that aren't good for your Kua number.

To calculate anyone's Feng Shui Kua number, you will need the following information:
- The year they were born that is the Birth Year
- Gender- Male/Female
- Convert DOB in Chinese calendar. Usually, February 4 is the Chinese new year.
- If you are born after February 4, consider your actual date of birth. Example: 20.06.2020, we will consider 2020 as the birth year.
- Born on 30.01.2021. Consider the year of birth one year prior, 30.01.2020

Kua Number Male
Before 2000
Step1- Take last two digits of Year from Date of Birth
Step 2 – Subtract it from 10
July 1956 = 5+6 = 11 = 2
10-2 = 8

On & After 2000:
Step 1 – remains same Step 2 – Subtract from 9
July 2021
2+1 = 3
9-3 = 6

If you get Kua number as 5, consider it as number 2 If your Kua number comes as zero, consider it as 9 **Female:**

Before 2000:
Step 1- Take last two digits of Year from Date of Birth
- Step 2 – We add to number 5

July 1956 = 5+6 = 11 = 2
2+5 = 7

On & After 2000
Step 1 – remains same
Step 2 – add to number 6
July 2021
2+1 = 3
3+6 = 9

If you get Kua number as 5, consider it as number 8

If your Kua number comes as zero, consider it as 9

Feng Shui Kua number & the two groups Kua Number divides people into 2 groups. The Feng Shui Kua Number divides people into East and West groups.

People, whose Kua number is 1, 3, 4, 9 or a 5 male belong to the East group.

Those, whose Kua number is 2, 6, 7, 8 or a 5 female belong to the West group.

Understanding one's Feng Shui Kua Number will help us determine the best areas for us and identify the best elements, lucky colors, lucky number, lucky seasons and lucky directions, thereby creating a positive mental attitude within ourselves.

This is a chart showing the Kua number compatibilities:

	Love	Friend	Neutral	Enemy
1	9	6 and 7	3 and 4	2 and 8
2	8	7	6 and 9	1, 3 and 4
3	7	4 and 9	1 and 8	2 and 6
4	6	3 and 9	1	2, 7 and 8
5 Male	8	7	6 and 9	1, 3 and 4
5 Female	2 and 9	6	3 and 7	1 and 4
6	4	1, 7 and 8	2	3 and 9
7	3	1, 2 and 6	8	4 and 9
8	2 and 9	6	3 and 7	1 and 4
9	1 and 8	3 and 4	2	6 and 7

Another chart depicting the relations between Kua numbers and directions for Money &Success, Health, Love & Marriage, and Spiritual Growth.

Kua Number	Money & Success	Health	Love & Marriage	Spiritual Growth
1	Southeast	East	South	North
2	Northeast	West	Northwest	Southwest
3	South	North	Southeast	East
4	North	South	East	Southeast
5 Female	Southwest	Northwest	West	Northeast
5 Male	Northeast	West	Northwest	Southwest
6	West	Northeast	Southwest	Northwest
7	Northwest	Southwest	Northeast	West
8	Southwest	Northwest	West	Northeast
9	East	Southeast	North	South

Chapter Thirteen

MEANING OF KUA NUMBERS

Kua Number 1
Component: Water

Harmonious with Black and Blue

Metallic and white are considered lucky colors.

Your element is water as your Kua number is 1. Wear hues that symbolise water, such as blue or black. Wear white or metallic to increase your luck since, according to Feng Shui, metal creates water.

Auspicious Directions for Kua Number 1:
Success: Southeast:

Plants with rounded leaves, such as money plants, should be positioned in this direction.

- Position a Chinese dragon so that it faces this way.
- Position a "Wealth Toad," a three-legged frog, facing this way. A coin ought to be in its mouth. Never let this frog face the front door.

Put a Laughing Buddha or any god who attracts prosperity here.

Health: East:

Put a Chinese dragon facing that way. But, avoid putting it in the bedroom.

Any type of water feature should be positioned in this direction. It aids in health improvement.

- Crystals should be hung or displayed in this direction to improve health.

Relationships: South:

Hang a picture of a phoenix to strengthen the bond.

To enhance romance in life, place pictures of peony flowers or a pair of Mandarin Ducks in this direction.

Wisdom: North:

This direction brings stability in life. Place a "Monkey Turtle" in this direction.

Statues of Elephants represent wisdom and steadiness.

Inauspicious Directions:

A common remedy to neutralize this effect is to use this area as little as possible.

Frustration: West:

Convert this area into a storeroom or toilet.

Never place any earth elements like crystals or clay pots in this area.

Display pictures of swimming fishes over here.

Loss/Theft: Northeast:

Put any brass object there, preferably a Brass Kuan Yin, and hang six I Ching coins on red threads to counteract the negativity.

Disease: Northwest:
- In this location, use precious gourds.
- Install an idol of the Eight Immortals here. It stands for prosperity and joy.

Total Loss: Southwest:
- Do not open any windows or doors that face this way. Keep them shut.
- To neutralize the negative energy, position a Laughing Buddha in this direction.

Kua Number 2
Element: Earth

Yellows and beiges are colors that go together (think "earth tones")

Colors that Bring Good Luck: blazing hues like red and purple

Your Kua number is 2, which indicates that earth is your element. Wear hues that reflect earth tones, such as beige or yellow. Fire creates earth according to Feng Shui, thus if you wish, Wear purple or red to increase your luck.

Auspicious Directions for Kua number2: Success: Northeast:
- When performing critical tasks, face this direction.
- Position images of carp fish in this way because they represent wealth.
- Position your head to face this way while yousleep.
- Clutter should not be present.
- The home's front door should face this way.

Health: West:

- Exquisite gourds stand for longevity and excellent health. In the northwest corner, hang these.
- Sleep with your head on this side. The bedroom should be located in the house's westernmost corner.

Relationships: Northwest:

Place a pair of Mandarin Ducks in this direction.

To symbolize healthy relationships, place a tortoise.

Wisdom: Southwest:

Place elephant statues.

Meditating in this corner will be beneficial.

Place a crystal globe in this area and give it a spin from time to time to activate personal growth.

Inauspicious Directions:

A common remedy to neutralize this effect is to use this area as little as possible.

Frustration: East:

Display pictures of mountains in this area.

No display of water feature

Avoid this area as much as possible.

Loss/Theft: Southeast:

Earth elements, like porcelain vases or clay figurines can be displayed here.

Place Kuan Kung and the four Heavenly Kings.

They protect from fraudulent people.

Disease: South:

The head should not be pointed in this direction while working or sleeping, and crystals should not be placed here.

Total Loss: North:

- Don't perform any actions in this direction.

- Avoid residing in a home with the main door facing in this direction.

No water feature should be positioned in this direction.

- If one must work in this direction, set up a statue of Kuan Kung in the background.

Kua Number 3:
Component: Wood:
Colors that go together: brown and green (think "trees")
Black and watery blue hues are lucky colors.
Auspicious Directions for Kua number3:
Success: South:
- Place a statue of horses on display, with golden ingots and I-Ching coins all around it.
- The front door of one's home or place of business should face this way.
- Position your head to sleep in this direction. To attract prosperity, face this way.

Health: North:
- Position your head to face this way while you sleep.
- Face any type of water feature,such as an aquarium, in thisdirection.

To improve the health circumstances, turn harmoniousturtles in this direction.

This fortunate direction improves interpersonal harmony.

Relationships: Southeast:
Puta pair of wooden Mandarinducks in this direction, as well as the Chinese scroll for love or theRose Quartz Crystal Ducks.

Put any type of green plant here.

Wisdom: East:
- Display pictures of the green dragon here.
- Install a water feature here.
- Increase your time spent here.
- Position your head to face this way while yousleep.
- Set up the Three Star Gods and Jade here.

Inauspicious Directions:

This unlucky direction brings misfortune and trouble. Negative energy makes things harder and makes things fail.

Frustration: Southwest:
- If there is a door or window in this direction, do not use it.
- Hang an I Ching Coin sword.
- Avoid putting any earthen or crystal elements inthis direction.

Loss/Theft: Northwest:
- Do not plant any flowersin this direction.
- Place a wind chime here.
- This region is perfect for installing a toilet.

I Ching Coins can be placed in this direction to counteract any negativeenergy.

Disease: Northeast:
- Keep aquariums away from this direction.

Temple Lions should be displayedin this direction.

If there is a bedroom in this direction, place six I-Ching coins there.

Total Loss: West:
- Avoid using the doors that face this direction if you live in a home with that orientation.

- Point a wind chime made of I-Ching coins in this direction.
- No water feature should be positioned in this direction.
- Position a pair of Fu Dogs so that they are facing this way.

Kua Number 4:
Element: Green:
Wood tones are the Harmonizing Colors (think "forest of trees")

Colors that Bring Good Luck: Black and wateryhues like blue

Success: North:
- If you're doing anything, turn yourhead in this way.
- To increase the positive energy,hang wind chimes (6 metal rods) in this direction.
- Face any water feature in this manner.
- Install Wealth Fish statues.

Health: South:
- If there is space, consider sleeping in this place toenhance your health.
- Put statues of Sau and Quan Yin, who represent enduring power.
- Utilize the doors that arepositioned in this manner.
You can also plant bright red flowers in this way.
- Evergreen plants improve the South's Fire element.

Relationships: East:
- Add a statue of a Chinese dragon or any other type of water element here.

- Improving relationships with coworkers will result from working in this area.
- Put a pair of Mandarin ducks there to improve your love life.

Wisdom: Southeast:
- Research in this area. Increase your time spent in this area.
- Place a statue of the WealthFish or the EightImmortals here.

Inauspicious Directions:

Frustration: Northwest:
- Set up a pair of Fu Dogs to counteract the bad energies of this direction.
- Never work sitting or facing this direction.
- Suspend crystal balls in this direction.

Loss/Theft: Southwest:
- Avoid working or spending time looking in this direction.
- Set up a Laughing Buddha or a Dragon Turtle here.

Disease: West:

A Lions Head plaque should be positioned in this direction.

No earth element should ever be placed in this direction.

To counteract its unfavorable vibe, make this place the restroom.

Total Loss: Northeast:
- Don't perform any work here.
- Add a statue of Kuan Kung or a windchime in this location.

Kua Number 5 (Male & Female):
Kua Number 5 Male
Element: Big Earth.
Yellows and beige are the Harmonizing Colors (think "earth tones")

Colors that Bring Good Luck: blazinghues like red and purple

Auspicious Directions for Kua Number 5 Male: Success: Northeast:
- This area needs to be maintained tidily.
- crystal balls should be placed to increase the impact of this direction.
- To attract money, the front door of your home and place of business should face this direction.

Health: West:
Toimprove your health,sleep with your headin this position. It will be advantageous to have the bedroomin this region of the house.

Toimprove health conditions, hang Wuloo or priceless gourds in this direction.

Relationships: Northwest:
- Position the turtle in this area. It stands for a healthy long life.
- Position the Mandarin Ducks in the bedroom or northwest corner of the building.

Wisdom: Southwest:
- Place any type of water element,such as a fountain or aquarium, at this position.

- Place a dragon turtle on display. It will offer security and safety.
- Spin a crystal globe every day while it is on display at this location.

Inauspicious Directions: Frustration: East:

- Convert this space to a pantry or kitchen.
- This space will be made active by a waterfeature. Hence, never position it in this manner.
- Avoid moving in that direction.

Loss/Theft: Southeast is the Direction:

- Point a statue of Kuan Kung in this direction. It will offer defense against treachery.
- Place earthy objects here, like earthenware and porcelain vases, to symbolise the earth. This reduces the area's negative energy.
- Working in this direction will result in loss, therefore avoid doing so.

Disease: South:

Build a storage space here, if you can, in the direction of the south. Use this region only as directed.

- Avoid sleeping in this direction because it could harm your health.
- Neither the entrance to the office nor the main door should face this direction.

Total Loss: North Overall Loss Direction

- Do not place any water feature in this direction or conduct any activity in this region.

Number 5 Kua (female)

Element: Earth:

Harmonizing colours: yellow and beige (think "earth tones")

Luck-Boosting Colors: flamboyant hues suchas scarlet and purple.

Success: Southwest:

- Display a picture of nine carp fish. It generates revenue.
- To activate the positive energy ofthis area, place riches symbols such as Pi Yao, coins set, and golden ingotsthere.
- Set up a three-legged frog exhibithere. It shouldn't, however, face the front door.

Health: Northwest:

- Turn this space into a bedroom. A healthy life willresult from it.

A tortoiseshould be positioned in this direction as it represents a healthy, long life.

Relationship: West:

Facing west in order to strengthen your bonds with others.

- Put a pair of Mandarin ducks there.
- Position images of peony blooms in this way as well.

Wisdom: Northeast:

- Set a crystal globe there to amp up the positive energy of this direction. Twirl it daily.

Inauspicious Directions for Kua Number 5Female

Frustration: South:

Do not use this area all that much

Put a crystal or semi precious stone to reduce thenegative energy.

Loss/Theft: North:

Place wooden objects to reduce the negative energy.

Avoid workingor sitting in the area.

Disease: East:

This direction is good for a storeroomor kitchen.

No waterfeature in this area.

Total Loss: Southeast:

Do not use this area.

If the main door of the house faces this direction then do not buy this property.

Hang a picture of a phoenix in this area. Kitchen or storeroom is okay over here.

Kua Number 6:

Element; Metal

White and Silver are the Harmonizing Colors(think "metallic")

Earth tones like yellows, beiges, taupe's, and purple are lucky colors

Success: West:

- Use this location for the office workstation to draw In additional income.
- The home's front door should face in this way.
- Use a three-legged frog to draw in additional business. It shouldn't be facing the entrance.

Health: Northeast:

If there is space, considersleeping in this portion of the house.

To enhance your health, place a crystal Lotus in this direction.

Relationships: Southwest:

To enhance partnerships, hang a pair of Mandarin Ducks or a Jade Double Happiness Charm in this location.

- Set a crystalglobe there and spin it.

Wisdom: Northwest:

From here, hang a wind chime using six metal rods.

Display a dragon turtle or a laughing Buddha in this direction.

Inauspicious Directions: Frustration: Southeast:

- There shouldn't be any clutter in this space.
- Kuan Kung's statue ought to be kept facing this way.
- Avoid placing a moving clock in this area as it will activate the negative energy.

Loss/Theft: East:

- Don't rest or do anything in this area.
- Set up a pair of Qi Lin in this location.

Disease: North:

- Avoid setting up your desk in this direction.
- Avoid putting in any water features.

Large, leafy plants should be positioned in this direction.

Total Loss: South:

- Avoid using anything that includes the fireelement. It stirs up the bad energy.
- Display items made of the element earth.

Kua Number 7:
Element: Metal:

Harmonizing Colors: White and Silver (think "metallic")

Luck-Boosting Earth tones including yellows, beiges, taupe's, and purple are used as colors.

Success: Northwest:

Both the front door of the house and the office should face this way. That will lead to achievement.

- Point a laughing Buddha or Chinese dragon in this direction.
- Work facing this direction or spend time in this direction.
- Set up a pair of Qi Lins facing this way.

Health: Southwest:

- Place your head in this direction
- Exhibit items made of earthy materials, such as pots or semiprecious stones.
- Use the door if it is facing this direction.
- Set a pair of Wuloo beside the bed.

Relationships: Northeast:

- Place a pair of Mandarin ducks in this position orhang a Chinese scroll depicting them.
- Jade or Rose Quartz Hearts. In addition, the Double Happiness Charm can be used.

Wisdom: West:

Place sculptures or paintings of tigers or elephants facing west in thisdirection.

You can also put the Tortoises of Harmony in this way.

Inauspicious Directions: Frustration: North:

- Keep clocks away from this location.
- Keep this space spotless.
- Tostop the bad energy, placea pair of Qi Lins or a Laughing Buddha there.

Loss/Theft: South:

- This area is not a good place to sleep.
- Set five crystal lotuses or clear crystal quartz semi-precious stones in this location.
- Maintain a clay pot loaded with rice in this location.
- Set up a statue of Quan Yin to counteract the bad energy.

Disease: Southeast:
- Avoid holding meetings while looking in this direction.
- Never open a door that faces in this direction to enter a home.
- Set up a statue of Kuan Kung to counteract the bad energy.

Total Loss: East:
- Avoid going in that direction.
- Include a kitchen in this space, if at all possible.
- Neither the front door of the house nor the office should face in this direction.

Kua Number 8
Element: Earth:
the colors yellow and beige are its harmonies (think "earth tones")

Luck-Boosting Colors: flamboyant hues such as scarlet and purple

Success: Southwest:
- Put a water feature or a group of six Happy Buddhas on display.
- To attract prosperity, hang a picture of nine carp fish.
- A three-legged rich toad should be positioned in this area.

Health: Northwest:

- Sleep with your head in this direction. It willbe most advantageous if there is a bedroom in this direction.
- The tortoise of Harmonystands for a long life and good health.

Relationships: West:

Put a pair of MandarinDucks towards the **direction of the west** to promoteromance.

- Peony flowers Image or Love Birds images can beposted if you're looking for love.

Wisdom: Northeast:

- A crystal globe should bepositioned in this area.
- Position a picture of the EightImmortals in this direction.

Inauspicious Directions: Frustration: South:

- This location shouldnot be used frequently
- Tolessen the negativeenergy, place a crystalorsome semi-precious stones in this direction.

Loss/Theft: North:

Put wooden objects in the **direction of the North**.

Avoid facing it while working, to lessen the effect of the negative energy.

Disease: East:

- The kitchen or a storeroom might benefit from this direction.
- A Temple Lion Protection Plaque should be hung there.

Total Loss: Southeast:

- Do not utilize this space in any way.

- Never purchase a home with the front door facing in this direction.
- Hang a photo of the Phoenix in this direction.
- A toilet, pantry, or kitchen can be built in this direction.

Kua Number 9:
Element: Fire:

Colors that are harmonious with Kua Number 9 include red, orange, and purple (think "fiery colors")

Luck-Boosting Woody hues like greensand browns are used as colors.

Auspicious directions for Kua number9

Success: East:
- The front door of the home should be facing this way.

Use this direction while working or sleeping.
- Point the Money Toad' or Horse of Successor in this direction.

Health: Southeast:
- Position a water feature in this direction, such as a fountain or an aquarium with 1 blackfish and 8 goldfish.
- Hang a crystalglobe.
- Plants with rounded leavesor a money plant should bepositioned in this direction.

Relationships: North:
- Position your head to face this way while yousleep.

Place a pair of Mandarin ducks or a Chinesescroll of Mandarin ducks to improve your love life.

Wisdom: South:
- Invest time in this area.

- Hang a picture of the Phoenix to activate the fire element.
- Position a group of elephants or a turtle with a dragon head in this way.

Inauspicious Directions: Frustration: Northeast

- When working or sleeping, avoid facing this way.
- Set up a pair of Qi-Linin this direction to lessen the impact of negative energy.
- Project a scene from nature in this direction.

Loss/Theft: West:

- Do not work facing this direction.
- To prevent dishonest coworkers, direct Kuan Kung or the Four Heavenly Kings in this direction.
- To protect against the negative energy, this space could be converted into a bathroom or a storage space.

Disease: Southwest:

- This space can be converted into a restroom or a storage room.
- Position a pair of Qi Lin in this manner.

Total Loss: Northwest:

- Don't stay here for too long.
- Showcase an aquatic feature.

To decrease the bad energy, hang gemstones in that direction.

Chapter Fourteen

FENGSHUI BAGUA MAP & ITS EFFECTS

"Numerical precision is the very soul of science." – D'Arcy Wentworth Thompson

WHISPERS OF THE LOSHU GRID

Feng Shui Bagua Map

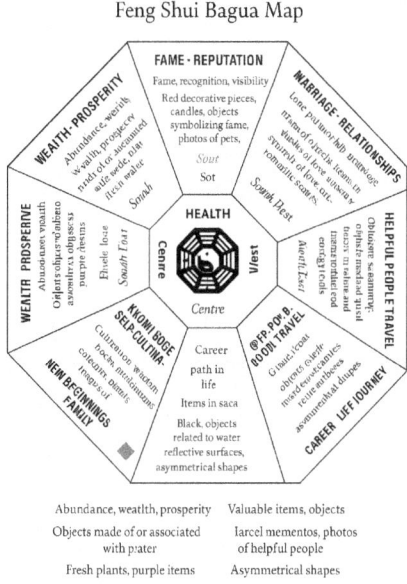

This is the most important symbol of Feng-Shui. The eight sides represents many things and above all it symbolizes a powerful protective energy. Chinese people hang this in front of their house, above the main door.

The effect of the missing directions depends on which direction is missing.

The Bagua assigns one type of luck to each of the eight directions of any residence.

When we superimpose the Lo Shu Grid on the Bagua, it is easy to understand the directions. The bagua can also be positioned on any floor plan and the missing directions can be found.

The diagram above illustrates the relationship between the eight-sided Pa-Kua and Lo-Shu magic square's nine grids. Please note that the Pa-Kua shown here places the direction of South at the top, to correspond with the number 9. This is because the Chinese compass places South at the top, and to ensure consistency and accuracy, it is necessary when relationships between symbols are being analyzed, and to comply with the practice followed in the ancient manuals.

Effects of the Missing Zone on Health:

SE MISSING	South missing	SW missing
Can be the cause of diseases related to the hips, liver, gallbladder, or thigh	Can be the cause of eye, heart, or digestion issues. Insomnia	Cause of stomach, spleen, pancreas or muscle joints issues
EAST missing	**CENTER missing**	**WEST missing**
Cause of feet, upper back, liver, and gallbladder issues	Diseases relating to stomach, liver, pancreas.	Issues related to lungs, mouth, skin, and hair.
NE missing	**NORTH missing**	**NW missing**
Cancer, stomach, hands, spleen related issues	Affects the ear, kidney, ovary, blood, fatigue, and knee	Affects the head, brain, and lungs

Effects of Missing Zones on Luck:

SE missing	South missing	SW missing
Affects wealth and luck. Income of the family is impacted negatively	Impacts name, fame, and recognition. The good name of the family could be spoiled	Adversely affects love, romance, and marriage.
EAST missing	**CENTER missing**	**WEST missing**
Affects family relationships and health. Causes illness and misunderstanding.	Completely empty or too heavy, both are not good	Diminishes the luck of the next generation. Luck of children is hampered.
NE missing	**NORTH missing**	**NW missing**
Knowledge is missing. Students appearing for exams or for job interviews will have no luck.	Career growth blocked	Help from mentor is absent.

Chapter Fifteen

PERSONAL YEAR GRID

"Numbers are a great way of organizing the universe." - Stephen Hawking

Using the Lo Shu grid, it is also possible to create a certain year's grid, compare it with the original grid and look for any missing or recurring energy.

How to Build one's Lo Shu Grid for a given year:

1. Put down your whole date of birth and make the original Lo Shu grid for use as a guide and point of comparison.

2. Create your grid based on the following information: Birthday (DD), Birth Month (BM), and Year in Question (2023 if this year is considered, the year in question is always taken from 1st January to 31st December).

3. Take note of the Personal Year Grid's missing and repeated numbers.

4. Provide solutions to improve a chart's flow while taking the controlling and producing cycle into account.

An illustration would be:

Original DOB for a Female: 27/05/1969
BD- 27/9 LP - 3
Kua Number - 11/2

	99	22
3	5	7
	1	6

For the shared example:

The person has only the 4 and 8 (Wood and Earth element respectively) missing in the original Lo Shu Grid, rest all elements are present while in the personal year chart of 2023, the numbers are like this:

BD - 27/9 PY - 3
KUA number - 2

	9	2222
33	5	7

4, 8, 1, and 6 are missing

8 being an earth element is getting support from 5 and 2. Ample support from 2. So, nothing to be done.

4 is getting support from 3, another wood element.

6 is also getting support from 7, another metal zone.

A person can improve 1 by being asked to wear blue-colored clothing, energize water in the North Zone in a blue bottle, and conserve water rather than waste it in any way.

Conclusion:

In this way, for a specific year, we may aid people and offer them cures to make it easier for them to handle their problems.

Chapter Sixteen

REMEDIES

"Numbers are a reflection of our thoughts, words, and deeds." - Unknown

Missing Earth Element:
- Place your office or bedroom towards the southwest.
- Employ a square or rectangular hardwood dining table.

Maintain a greenstone pyramid in the southwest for steadiness and strength.

- Attach a mountain photo on the south sidewall of your home.
- Place a yellow light bulb in the room's middle.

Put natural crystals in the northeast and southwest.

- Granite glass pebbles

Any sort of red, orange, and yellow fruit is great for soil because fire creates it.

Missing Metal Element:
- Accessorize your right hand with gold.

- Place a wind chime in the west, northwest, or north. It should be golden yellow.
- Keep bronze, silver, or gold metal statues in the west or northwest.

Colors of metallic colors, such as whites and golds, look fantastic here when paired with earth tones.

Wind chimes are terrific here since they bring down bad luck and also bring good luck.

Missing Water Element:
- Maintain a basin of water towards east or northeast.
- Offer water to thirsty people. You can also keep a fish aquarium with water.
- A fountain or swimming pool will also be useful in the north.
- Water should never flow outward from a home, only inward.
- Even though your bed room is in the north, a water feature is not appropriate there.
- The north-facing area of another room can always be powered up.

Maintain a red lamp in the southeast corner of your room.

Missing Fire Element:
- Place a flowering plant in your living room.
- Position the oven so it faces southeast.

Maintain an energetic red pyramid. Green and red make a fantastic color combination.

Missing Wood Element:
- Place musical doorbell chimes at the front door.
- Maintain order and cleanliness in your home's northeast side.
- Install a green light facing east and south.
- On the east, southeast, and northeast, hang a picture of some greenery;
- Surround yourself with plants and wooden items.

Remedies in details for missing numbers in the Lo Shu grid:

The table below can help you to fix the missing numbers in your Lo Shu grid

No.	Direction	Element	Solution
1	North	Water	Put a water fountain or aquarium. Hang a painting or a picture of flowing water in a metal frame. Hang a light mirror or a wall clock. Replica of Kan diagram
2	Southwest	Earth	Hang a picture of mountains without water. Wear a necklace of pearls or crystals. Keep a pair of crystal balls, birds, or flowers. Keeping Amethyst/Rose quartz rocks or wearing a pendant. Bracelet with these stones will be very helpful in strengthening relationships. Keep a stone pyramid. Replica of Kun trigram.
3	East	Wood	Keep energized green stone pyramid. Put a small green plant or green bulb. Put a picture of greenery/green plants. Put a green octagonal pyramid. Keep a wooden pen, wooden key ring, etc. with you. Put a wooden wall clock on the East wall. (octagonal shape). Replica of Chen trigram
4	Southeast	Wood	Keep a picture of greenery. Keep energized green stone pyramid. Light a green bulb, put up images of green trees. Sun trigram with you

WHISPERS OF THE LOSHU GRID

			Keep an energized green pyramid in the Southeast direction of the bedroom. Keep a wooden pen, wooden key ring, etc.
5	Center	Earth	Hang high peak mountain poster without water. Wear a crystal pendant. Wear a pearl ring. Keep a stone pyramid Hang a yellow bulb in the center of the room. Wear crystals in any form or shape. Hang a crystal chandelier or crystal balls.
6	Northwest	Metal	Wear a watch with a golden metallic chain. Hang 6 rod metal wind chime. Install energized white or metallic pyramids. Wear a yellow or golden armlet Wear a watch with a golden metal chain Put up a golden wind chime with 6 rods. Keep a white or golden octagonal pyramid. Picture of Chien Trigram.
7	West	Metal	Wear a watch with a golden metallic chain. Hang 7 rod metal wind chime. Install energized white or metallic pyramids. Wear a white silver armlet Wear a wristwatch with a silver metal chain Put up a silver wind chime with 7 rods. Keep a white or silver octagonal pyramid. Replica of Tui Trigram
8	Northeast	Earth	Wear a necklace or pendant of crystals. Keep a crystal lotus or anything of crystal. Picture of Ken diagram.
9	South	Fire	Install energized pyramid. Put a red bulb in the South direction. Or keep a red pyramid. Picture of Li Trigram

Matching the element of that direction with the proper things, forms, or colors and placing them in that zone is the quickest and easiest approach to activate each area.

Plants for the Southeast and East:

The east and southeast bring excellent health and riches, respectively. Choosing plants with robust, succulent leaves that resemble the wood element is a good idea. Blue carpets, wall paper, or cushions are also appropriate because they symbolize water, which is said to "create wood" figuratively.

Utilize crystals for the Southwest, Northeast, and Center.

Love and romance are brought by the southwest, academic success is symbolized by the northeast, and family luck is found in the center. Place natural crystals in these three sections since they represent the earth element. Things like these include glass, stones, pottery, and granite. Any item with red, or yellows and oranges are ideal for earth sectors since earth is produced by fire in the five element cycle.

Utilize Water for the North:

Nevertheless, don't go overboard. Water features in the north provide career luck. Although drinking too much water might be harmful, doing it in moderation can bring great fortune because water is a sign of money. Even though your bedroom is in the north, water features are inappropriate there since it should always flow inward towards the residence. Invigorate the north area of a different room that you use regularly instead. The colors black, blue, and white represent the metal element, which supports water, making this an ideal color combination (blue or black).

Apply Lights to the South:

Bright lights and crystals will make this are exciting because the fire element in the south is associated with fame, luck, and respect. Green and red are a fantastic color combination from a Feng Shui standpoint, but if you think they're too jazzy," just lighten the hues. Colors don't have to be vibrant to stimulate an aspect.

Utilize metal for the Northwest and West. The northwest and west are said to offer luck and good fortune to the family patriarch, respectively. Wind chimes are great because they bring down bad luck while also energizing good luck in this situation. As they move with the wind and make noise, more Yang energy is produced. Here, metallic hues, whites, and golds look excellent, especially when paired with earth tones. One word of warning You can energize all the sectors, but a word of caution: avoid over-energizing any one sector by having too much of the specific element required, as this might lead to imbalance and be hazardous.

Chapter Seventeen

NUMBER COMBINATIONS

"Numbers are a reflection of our thoughts, words, and deeds." - Unknown

Career /Profession – Number

One or two of these numbers should be present in a birth grid of a person.

Architect 1,4,5,8

Artist 2,6

Occult Sciences (Astrology etc.) 4,5.7,8

Advertisement 1,5

Automobile 4

Acting 2,6,7,9

Aluminum 5

Beauty Products1,2,6,3

Banking 3,2,5

Beauty Parlor 6,2

Bakery 2,6

Book Shop 3,5
Mobile Phone 4,5
Chemical Products 2,9,8,7
Computer Business 1,2,8,9,5
Construction 1,5,9
Cement 4,7,8
Clothing 3,2,6
Catering 6,2,9,5
Departmental Stores 1,9,2
Dairy Products 2,6
Electrical 1,9,4
Education/Counselling/Spiritual 3,2,5
Engineering 4,5,8,9
Import Export 1,2,7
Fast Food 9,2,6
Fashion 1,2,7,6
Finance related profession 3,9,5
Dress Making 2,3,5,6
Gold Shop 2,3,5,6
Lawyer 1,2,5,7
Stock Market 3,5
Politics 1,4,9

Ready Reckoner of Kua Numbers: Born between 1926 and 2026

Year of Birth	Male	Female	Year of Birth	Male	Female
1926	2	4	1971	2	4
1927	1	5	1972	1	5
1928	9	6	1973	9	6
1929	8	7	1974	8	7
1930	7	8	1975	7	8
1931	6	9	1976	6	9
1932	5	1	1977	5	1
1933	4	2	1978	4	2
1934	3	3	1979	3	3
1935	2	4	1980	2	4
1936	1	5	1981	1	5
1937	9	6	1982	9	6
1938	8	7	1983	8	7
1939	7	8	1984	7	8
1940	6	9	1985	6	9
1941	5	1	1986	5	1
1942	4	2	1987	4	2
1943	3	3	1988	3	3
1944	2	4	1989	2	4
1945	1	5	1990	1	5
1946	9	6	1991	9	6
1947	8	7	1992	8	7
1948	7	8	1993	7	8
1949	6	9	1994	6	9
1950	5	1	1995	5	1
1951	4	2	1996	4	2
1952	3	3	1997	3	3
1953	2	4	1998	2	4
1954	1	5	1999	1	5
1955	9	6	2000	9	6
1956	8	7	2012	6	9
1957	7	8	2013	5	1
1958	6	9	2014	4	2
1959	5	1	2015	3	3
1960	4	2	2016	2	4
1961	3	3	2017	1	5
1962	2	4	2018	9	6
1963	1	5	2019	8	7
1964	9	6	2020	7	8
1965	8	7	2021	6	9
1966	7	8	2022	5	1
1967	6	9	2023	4	2
1968	5	1			
1969	4	2			
1970	3	3			

Chapter Eighteen

About the Author

Lipiie Banerjjee

Lipiie Banerjjee's life has been a journey shaped by curiosity, courage, and a deep desire to understand the hidden patterns of the universe. Born in Kolkata, India, , then she spends her first 10 years of life in Madhya Pradesh, now called Chhattisgarh, and then moved to Kolkata again. Lipiie embraced the nomadic life of an explorer, moving across India with her husband and children. In every city they called home, she built not just a household, but a sanctuary of learning and growth.

A lifelong learner, Lipiie pursued a diverse range of studies—from a Diploma in Special Education to certifications in Parenting, Transactional Analysis, Neuro Linguistic Programming (NLP), and Reiki. Her thirst for knowledge didn't stop there. Today, she continues her academic journey, working towards a Ph.D. from the University of Metaphysical Sciences, California.

Now based in Mumbai, with her children having flown the nest, Lipiie balances her spiritual pursuits with her role as co-founder of a thriving Software and BPO company she established with her brother. It was during her Personal Year "5," a time marked by change and adventure in numerology, that she was drawn to the mysteries of the Occult.

Eventually, she embraced her destiny number "3"—a path that led her to become a passionate teacher and trainer in Numerology and Astrology. Through her work, she not only shares knowledge but also empowers others to uncover their soul's blueprint. She also continues to train in NLP, refining her skills to communicate transformation in the most effective ways.

Her Personal Year "3"also sparked a new passion: writing. Fueled by the frustration of trying to piece together scattered information on the internet and inspired by years of teaching, Lipiie began crafting her own method. This book is the result—a culmination of her learning, teaching, and experience. It is designed as a practical and accessible handbook for both her students and her clients.

The concept of *Trigram Therapy* emerged organically from her consultations, as she witnessed its positive impact firsthand. Over time, she integrated elements such as the Kua Number and basic Feng Shui, recognizing their relevance in everyday life. Her approach is holistic, intuitive, and rooted in real-world application.

Lipiie draws inspiration and gratitude from many sources and acknowledges key references that shaped her understanding, including:

- *The Magic Square of Three in Old Chinese Philosophy and Religion* by Schuyler Cammann

- *Hidden Meaning of Numbers* by Tom Muldoon
- *The Magic Lo Shu Grid* by Pt. Gopal Sharma and Dr. Sewaram Jaipuria

A writer, teacher, guide, and healer, Lipiie Banerjjee is active on social media and regularly shares insights on her website, offering a space for seekers to grow and evolve.

Connect with her here:

Website: https://lipibanerjee.com/

Facebook: Growth Synergist

Instagram: @lipiiebanerjjeegrowthsynergist

Email:banerjeelipi121@gmail.com

www.ingramcontent.com/pod-product-compliance
Lightning Source LLC
Chambersburg PA
CBHW050342010526
44119CB00049B/662